MW00996354

ABOUT THIS BOOK

A book about User Experience Design should be like the approach it advocates: User Friendly with functional visuals that makes for an easy "navigation". This book is heavily packed with small bites of information every UX Designer should know.

The book visually presents the most important definitions, methods and techniques for an easy to follow and immersive experience. My hope is that it will become the go-to dictionary for every designer, thanks to its well organized format.

UX BITES starts by defining the meaning and value of User Experience Design and presents the most efficient workflows of the UX process. It then makes a case for adopting a user-centric approach, while helping the reader master ways to understand their user. Presenting frequently used research methods, and explaining how to apply each, it prepares the reader to take real UX projects head on. The final two chapters move the spotlight to practical tips and statistics every designer can apply, and as a conclusion, it ends highlighting unethical practices to avoid as a UX Designer.

ABOUT THE AUTHOR

It makes me so happy that you are here, reading this! Hi! My name is Gabriel, I'm a UX Designer and Consultant. I've worked on larger enterprise projects that became successful and well funded, but also on startups that have never seen the light of day. I am at my second design company, because the first one failed miserably, so my background is of a human's with its wins and losses.

In this book I will share my experience in UX Design, but I will also often quote leaders of the industry and present universal rules and methods of this beautiful and relatively new discipline.

My motto is "Usability testing is the best way to argue with yourself" and I strive to remember and live by this, putting my ego aside every time I step into a new project.

I am the captain of the ship called @uxbites, a UX Design community on Instagram, where I try to share value to curious and like-minded designers. Come say Hi there, and let me know what you think of this book!

LET'S GET STARTED

SUMMARY

DEFINING

USER EXPERIENCE **DESIGN**

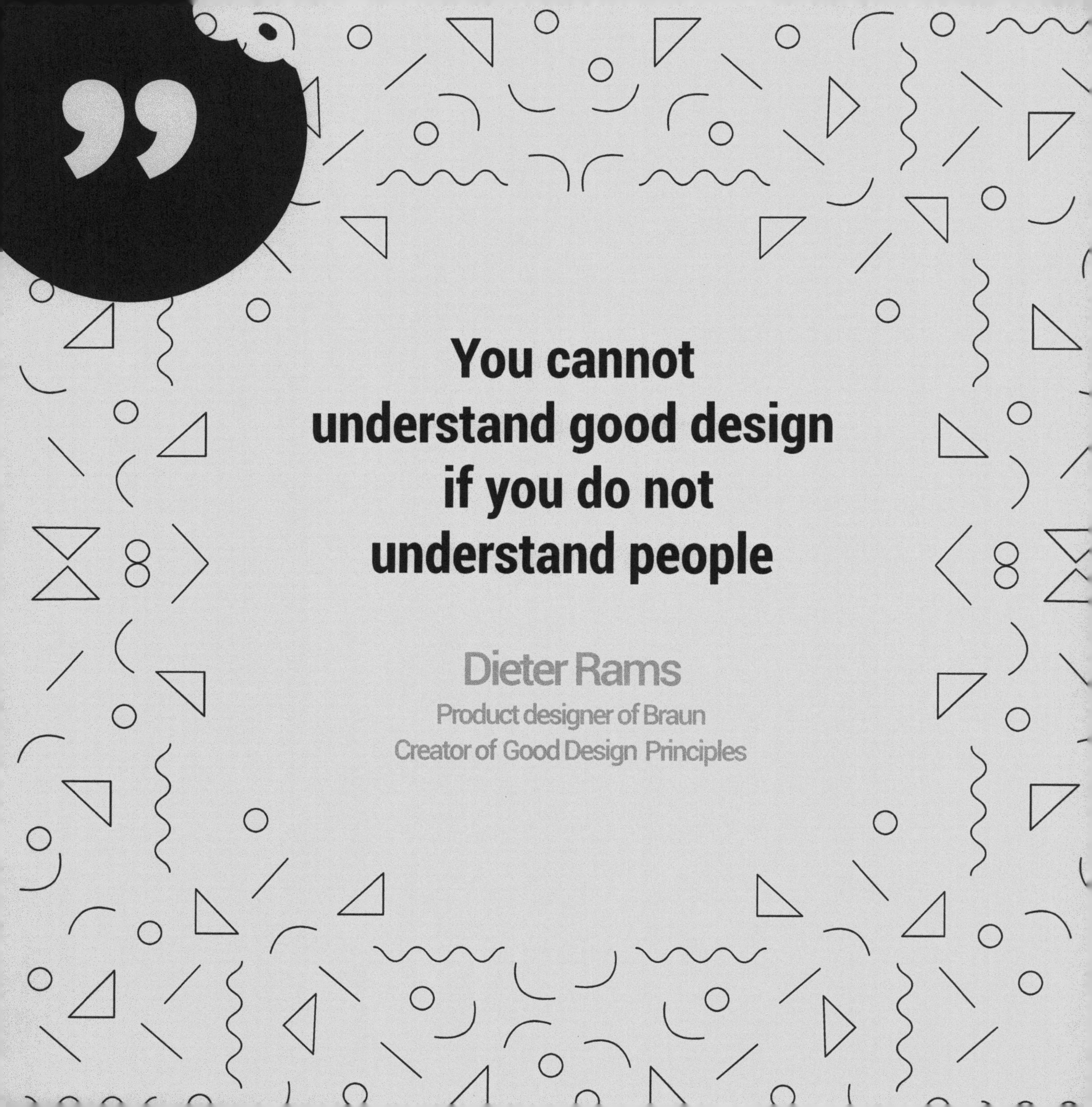
You cannot
understand good design
if you do not
understand people
Dieter Rams
Product designer of Braun
Creator of Good Design Principles

WHAT IS
USER EXPERIENCE DESIGN

The name User Experience Design is fairly suggestive, yet people often raise their eyebrows when they hear it.
If we abbreviate it to UX Design, even more so.
Shorten it again - UX - and now it sounds really technical!

It contains the word Design, yet it's so much more than that. Research, User Interface or customer experience are also subsets of UX Design.

Although the quote on the left is from a legendary industrial designer, I think it's the perfect representation of the main goal of UX: understanding the user. UX Design has a very clear purpose, to make people's life better with digital products that assists their life. The only way to do that is by understanding the user's needs. Happily, this profession has all the instruments that are necessary in this regard.

In this chapter we'll go deep into defining what User Experience Design actually is. Let's dig in!

ITERATIVE

USER
CENTRIC

UX

USABILITY
CENTRIC

BASED
ON DATA

DEFINING UX DESIGN

It should be clarified from the beginning that UX Design is not an art form. It's a fairly technical data and empathy driven approach to better understand the target user's desires and needs. This naturally results in an easier adoption of your project. UX Design is well fitted for any profession (I remember someone asking me how they could apply UX thinking in agriculture), but it's most commonly used with digital products and this book is focusing solely on that.

UX Design is User-centric. In fact, this is how it was first called, before Don Norman defined the term User Experience Design, in the book "The Design of Everyday Things". Being user-centric is the biggest switch from the product-centric approach we had before. Don Norman, while working on Apple, realized that people should have a better experience throughout the whole shopping flow. When they take the product out of the box, when they first boot it or when they just look at it for the first time.

UX design is also data driven. It tries to avoid building products on assumptions as much as possible. Instead, UX professionals make decisions on data earned from different research methods, which we are going to talk about later.

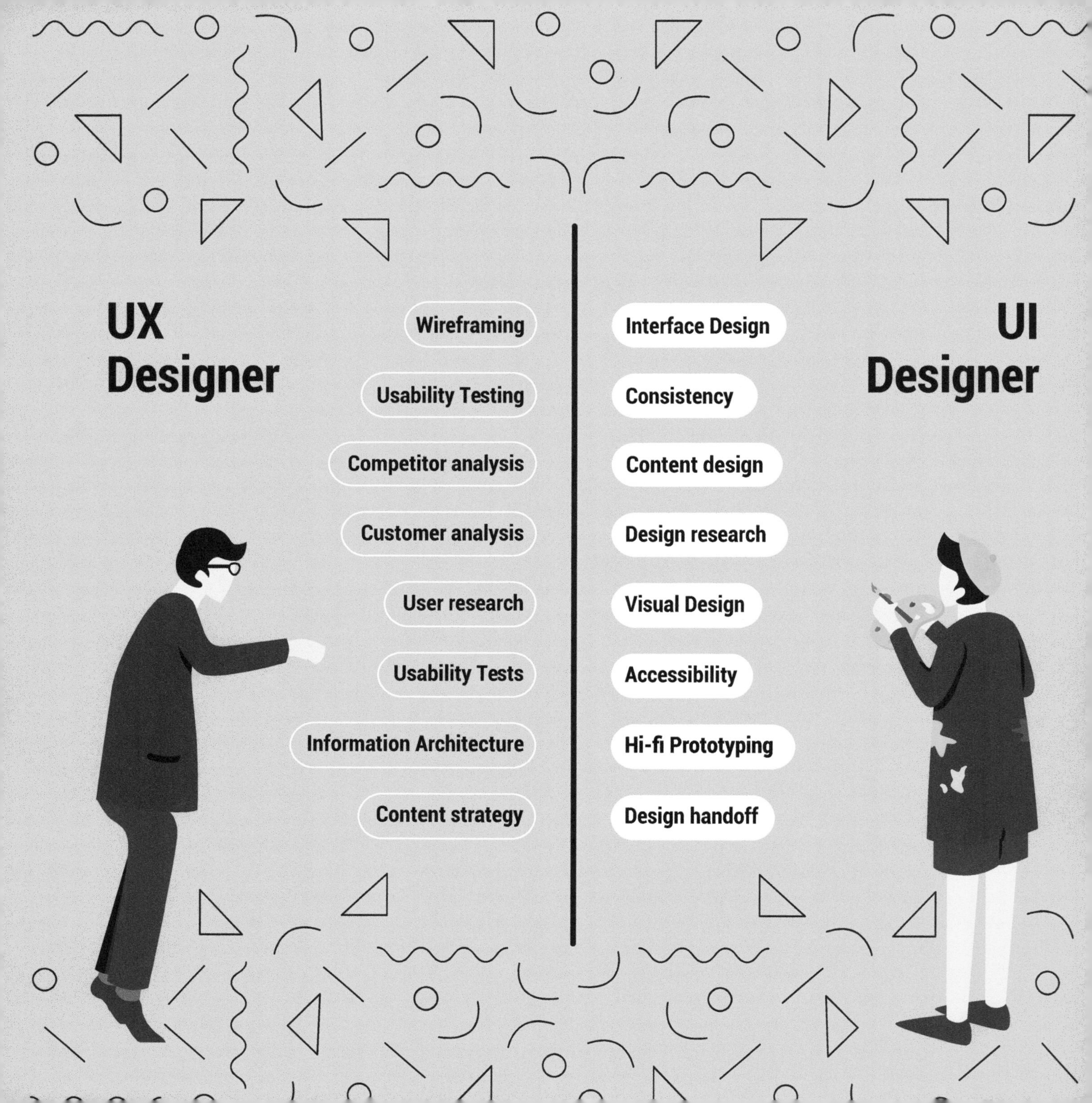
UX
Designer
Wireframing
Usability Testing
Competitor analysis
Customer analysis
User research
Usability Tests
Information Architecture
Content strategy
UI
Designer
Interface Design
Consistency
Content design
Design research
Visual Design
Accessibility
Hi-fi Prototyping
Design handoff

UX DESIGN ≠ UI DESIGN

This is an important distinction to make. Although a person can be both UX and UI Designer, they are two separate area of focus, even if they are very well connected. Some aspects of a healthy UX Design process should precede any kind of UI work. UX Designers first need to discover who are the target user and what are their pain points that could be solved by a product. Later, when sufficient data is gathered, and the UI process can start, the UX Designer needs to focus on maintaining a high rate of usability, while the UI Designer works on high fidelity prototypes.

A UX Designer tries to discover, understand and solve the target user's biggest frustrations. Their main focus is providing value to the user.

A UI Designer takes the strategy laid out by the UX Designer and tries to offer a consistent and easy flow for the user, while always taking accessibility into consideration.
The UI Designer is also the one making sure that design hand off to developers is successful. UI Designers work closely together with Developers, making sure they have everything they need to recreate the layouts provided.

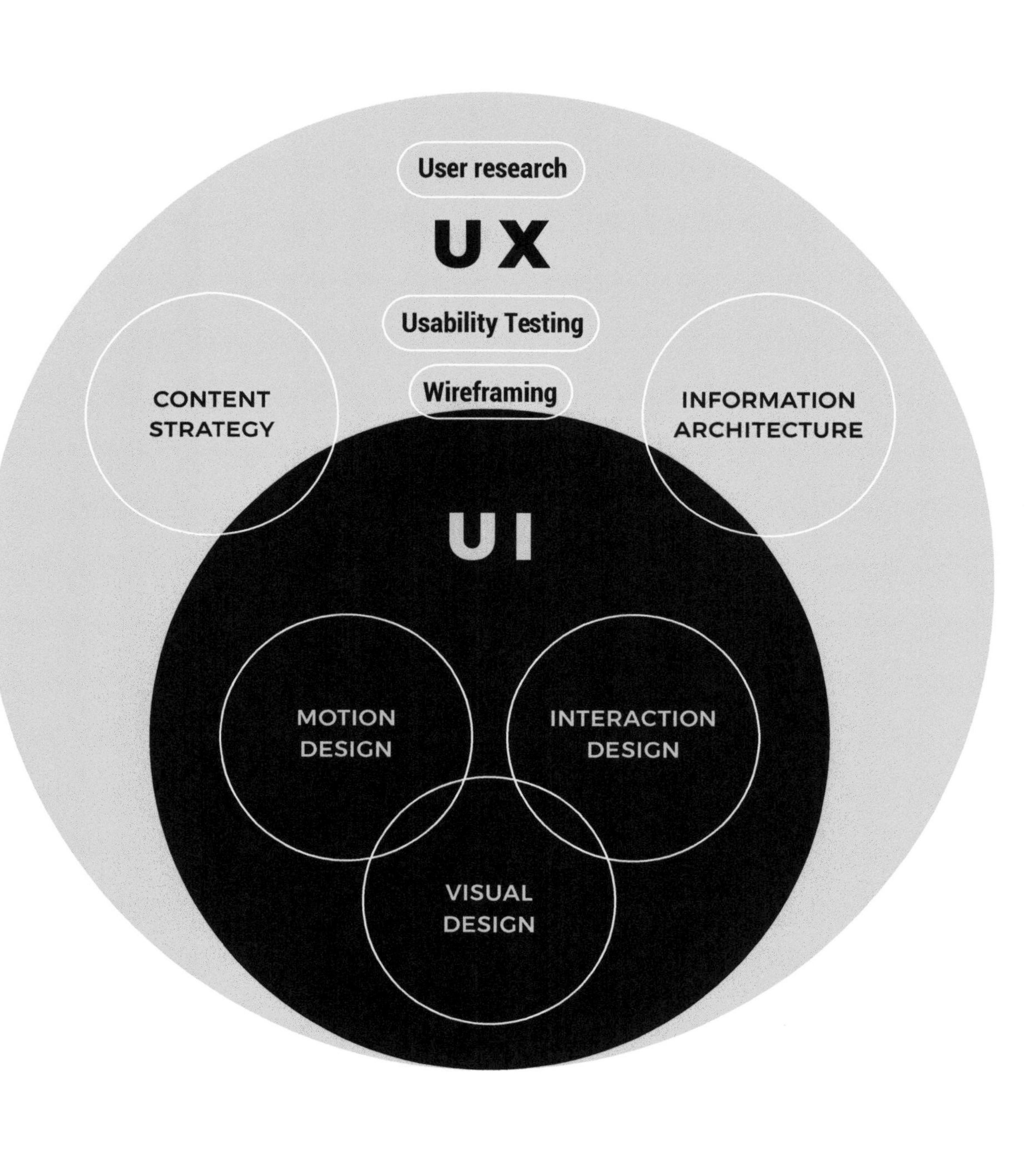
User research
UX
Usability Testing
Wireframing
CONTENT
STRATEGY
INFORMATION
ARCHITECTURE
UI
MOTION
DESIGN
INTERACTION
DESIGN
VISUAL
DESIGN

UX AS A BIGGER UMBRELLA

Getting closer to defining User Experience Design, we find out it's an umbrella for many aspects.

UX Design consists of User Research, Usability Analysis and Testing, Wireframing and Information architecture. Content strategy is also part of UX Design, even if it's often ignored, which is really a shame because most of the Usability issues discovered could be solved with better copy.

User Interface design consists of Motion, Interaction and Visual Design. As you can see, the User Interface is actually a subset of UX, but that doesn't make it less important. As you go further in this book, you'll discover how powerful a good UI is or how unfunctional a digital product would be without motion. But until then, just keep this in mind: 94% of first impressions of a product are made based on the visual aspect only!

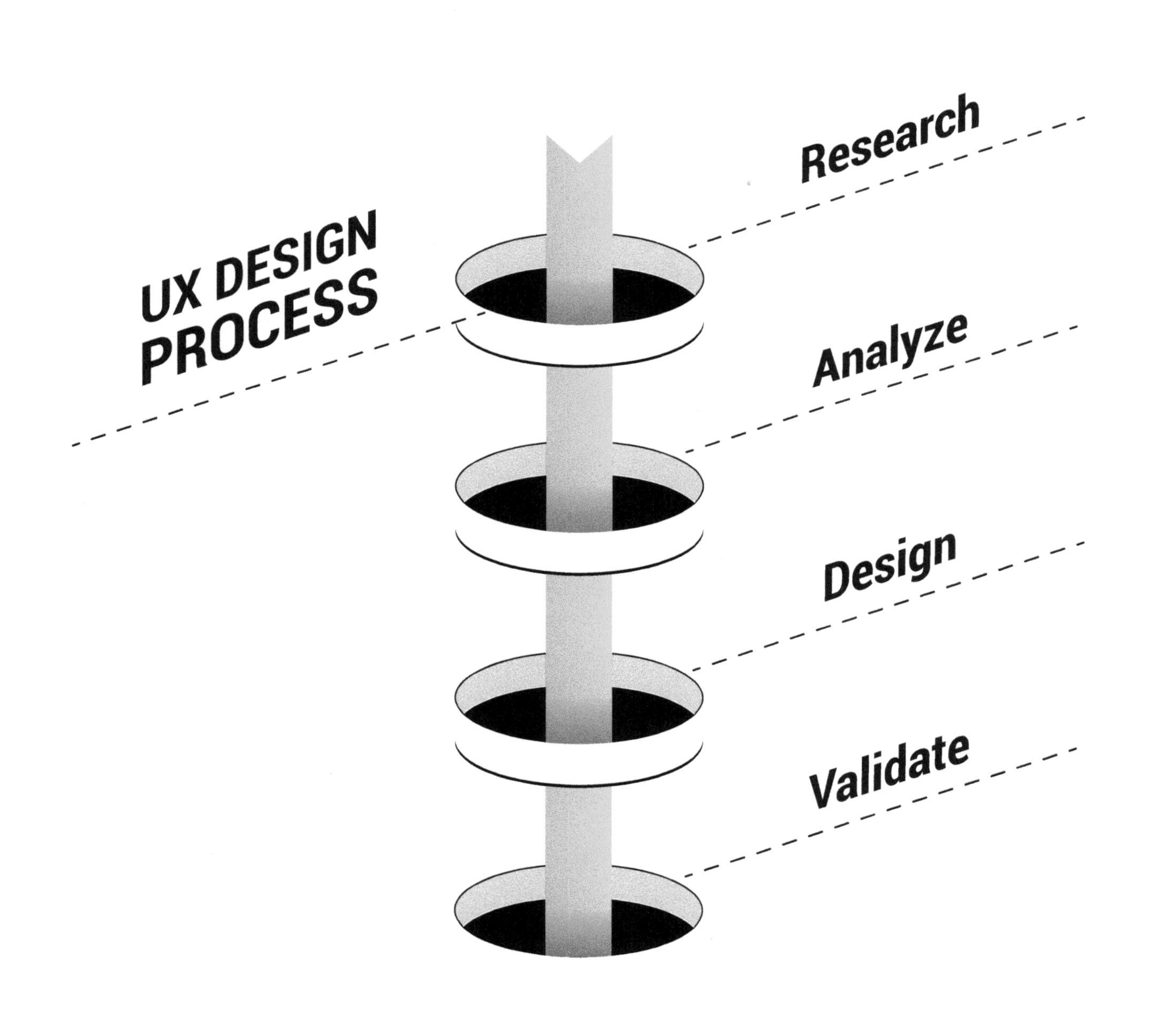
UX DESIGN
PROCESS
Research
Analyze
Design
Validate

THE FOUR STEPS OF ANY SUCCESSFUL UX DESIGN

UX Design takes time! Months, sometimes years pass between the start and the release date of a product. So it's naturally based on a process that can be used as an anchor along the way. What's great about this process is that it can be applied on a macro level, considering the whole project, but it also can be derived to every small feature you might add or improve to your project.

The process starts with discovering who are the target user, what defines them and what frustrates them in the context of your project. This knowledge is gathered with different research tools. Next step is analyzing the gathered data and defining the product based on that. Then we move towards designing the product, again, based on what we learned about the user, and not based on assumptions. Even if we went through a rigorous research phase, we still need to validate what we came up with, which is the fourth and last step of the process. Let's dig deeper into each one in the next couple of pages.

UX DESIGN PROCESS

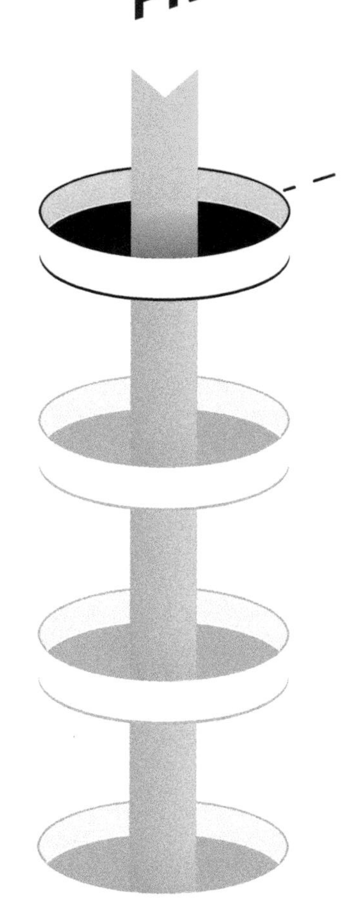

Research

Competitor analysis,
User interviews,
Surveys

STEP 1: RESEARCH

Simply put, UX Design tries to solve problems the user is facing. But what are those problems? And who is the user exactly? What defines them? All these questions can be answered only by research. Now research sounds very technical and scientific, but with a little preparation it's actually a logical and approachable tool that can help any designer to create successful products.

Opinions around terminology are divided. I prefer to call it the first step of the UX Process because the work around it is made with research methods. But it can also be called the Discovery phase and some might say it's more accurate because there are research methods applied throughout the whole UX Process. I prefer to call it Research to highlight the importance of user interviews, field studies and other initial research methods. So let's call this step Initial Research to please everybody!

UX DESIGN PROCESS

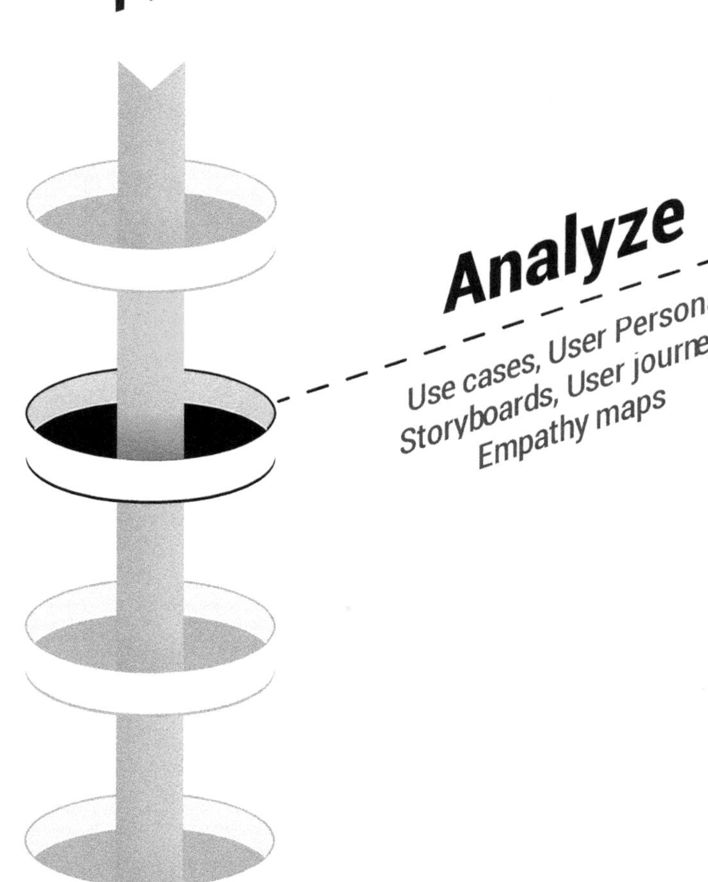

STEP 2:
ANALYZE

We are done with our research, but what we achieved from it is raw data, and that's exactly what the next step of the UX Design process tries to make sense of.

This step is crucial because at the end it will define the value of the project. You might start a project because you think that you found a great value that improves a specific user group's life. But these first two steps can validate that hypothesis or sometimes make it obsolete. So in UX, in general, but especially when analyzing raw data, it's very important to do that in a controlled and unbiased manner. In order to avoid biased decisions, try to define your users by their behavior and attitude. Including people from different backgrounds and characteristics will result a complete image.

The methods of how to analyze and how to draw conclusions from research data are detailed later.

UX DESIGN PROCESS

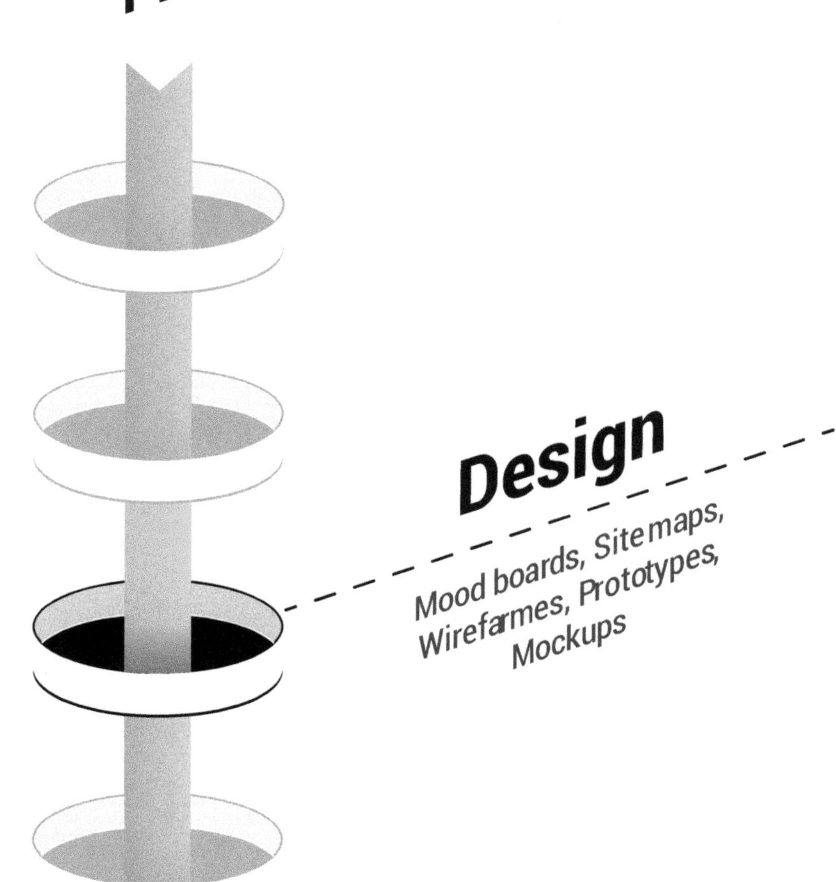

STEP 3: DESIGN

Research and analysis gave us a clear direction on what a product needs to achieve in order to be useful for the target audience. Now it's time to put this knowledge in practice, with the help of Design.

I think it's safe to say that the design phase is the step most of us enjoy the most. But the problem with many projects, and this is usually due to client pressure, is that many designers are forced to jump into design, skipping altogether the first two crucial steps of defining the actual problems.

Keep in mind that visual appearance is extremely important, but functionality and consistency should always conquer over how beautiful a UI is. Do you find the layout of Amazon the modern and cutting edge design? Probably not. But it's the constantly improved usability aspect that makes it a great product.

UX DESIGN PROCESS

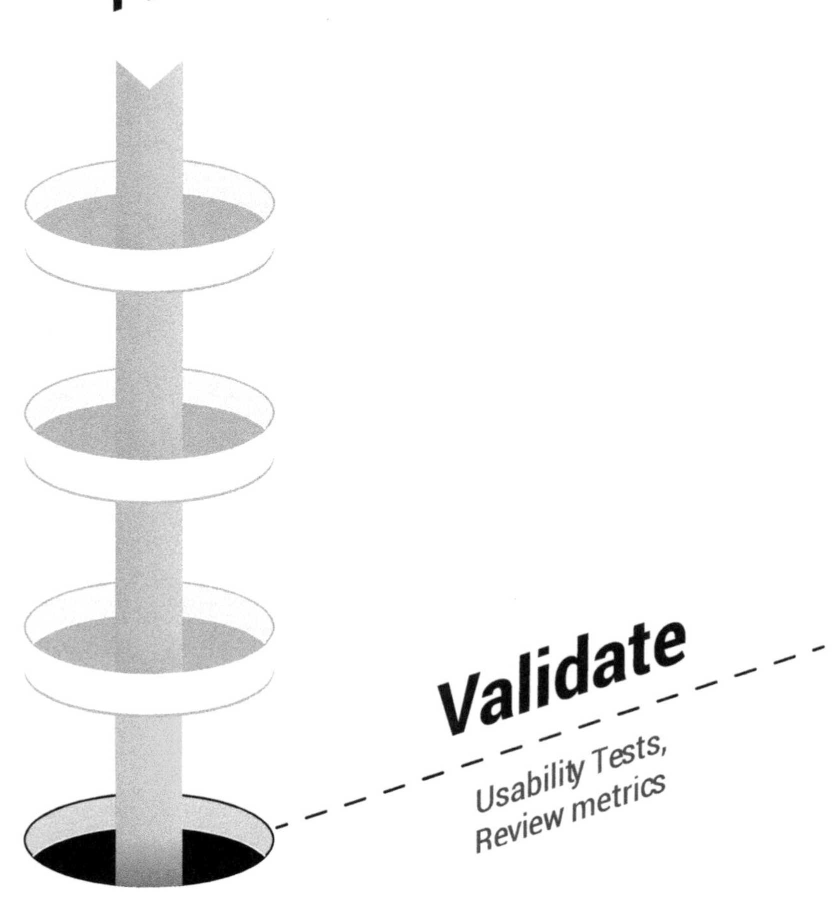

STEP 4: VALIDATE

We worked so much already! We researched, analyzed and designed an apparently great project or feature. But the truth is we still can't be sure if our approach makes sense to the users we want to target.

That's why the fourth and last step of a successful UX Design process is Validating our designs. This means giving it into our target's hands and observe how well they can reach their goals. The best tool for this is Usability testing, later detailed in the book.

Here's how the whole UX Design process becomes iterative. If the user successfully interacts with the product and they receive value from it, it's great news, the UX process was a success. But if other issues arise, the whole process starts over again to build upon the current version, improving it based on the user's feedback.

reasons a user opens an app

OR A BROWSER

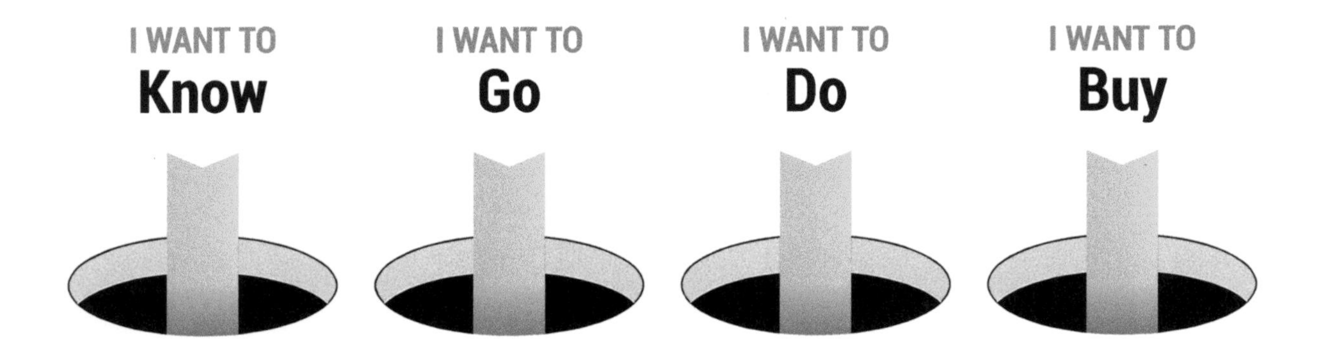

UNDERSTAND THE REASON A USER TAKES AN ACTION

I will mention Dieter Rams again, a great industrial designer from Braun, and you could argue that he's the main inspiration for the most famous Apple products. He said "Good design is invisible". That means that an interface shouldn't draw the user's attention on itself, but on the value it offers and the functionalities to achieve that value. This is why Google was so successful from the beginning, it's just a search bar, and nothing else distracts you from the purpose you opened up the page in the first place.

So, behind every visit on a platform there's a reason. These reasons can be placed in just four categories. Users either want to know, go, do or buy. This is important to realize, because only if you know why a platform is visited, you can make sure that you help the user in any possible way to achieve the goal of their visit.

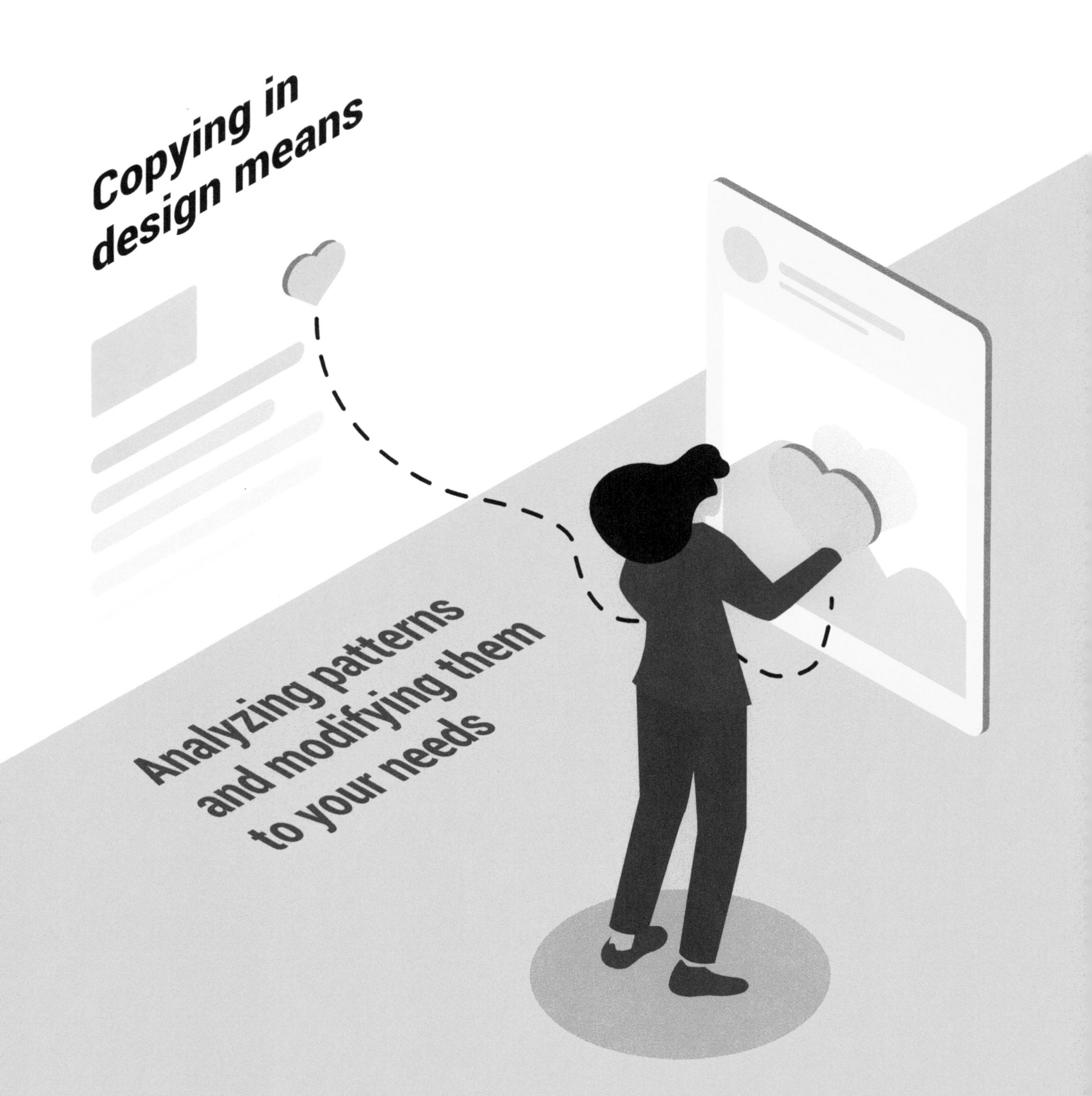
Copying in
design means
Analyzing patterns
and modifying them
to your needs

INSPIRATION IN UX DESIGN OR HOW TO STEAL SMART

How can a UX Designer be inspired to find solutions and create usable products?
When you look at your most commonly used platforms, they are fairly similar. Every solution seems to be adopted by other platforms already. Reinventing the wheel all the time won't fit well with the mental models of your potential customers.

But remember, your platform is different from all the other ones. Be curious, analyze and question every single decision other companies made in a product, so you can understand the logic behind it and see if it fits your needs and how.

Great designers don't copy, but analyze common patterns and shape those to fit their context.

3 WAYS DESIGN CAN MAKE YOU HAPPY

THE REFLECTIVE WAY — It became part of my identity

THE BEHAVIORAL WAY — I can master it, makes me feel smart

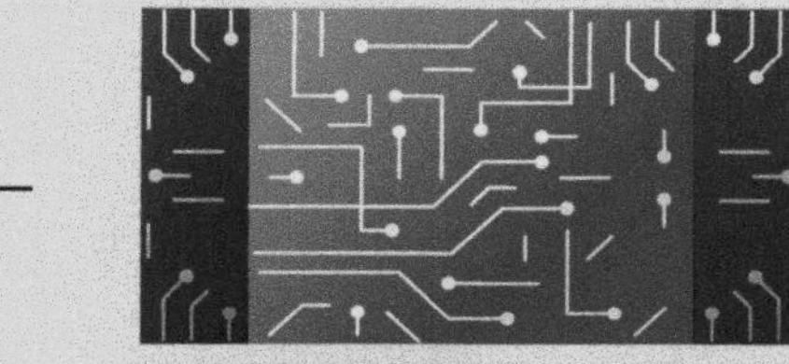

THE VISCERAL WAY — It looks beautiful, I want it!

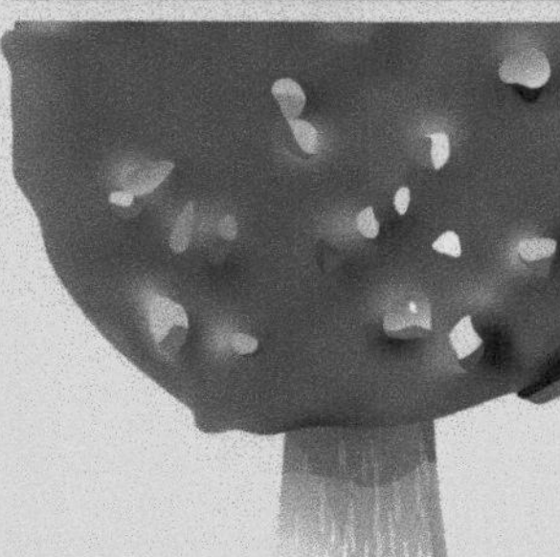

HOW DESIGN CAN MAKE YOU HAPPY

Every designer needs to ask himself how to create a product that will be adopted by the user. Adoption is something you will keep hearing in this exciting field and it's essentially the most important factor to consider in any new decision.

Don Norman conceptualized how a product can make you happy, and to achieve that, these are the three levels a product should thrive for.

The first interaction with a product is often called visceral and it refers to how an object make a person feel. Because products within the same category usually offer the same features, the visceral level is the first perception that tells two products apart.

The behavioral level refers to the efficiency of a product. A user should feel a sense of achievement using a product, feeling that they can master it.

The reflective level is the highest level of emotional design and it's achieved when a user is proud to own a product and associate their identity with it.

HOW WE MAKE

Decisions in UX

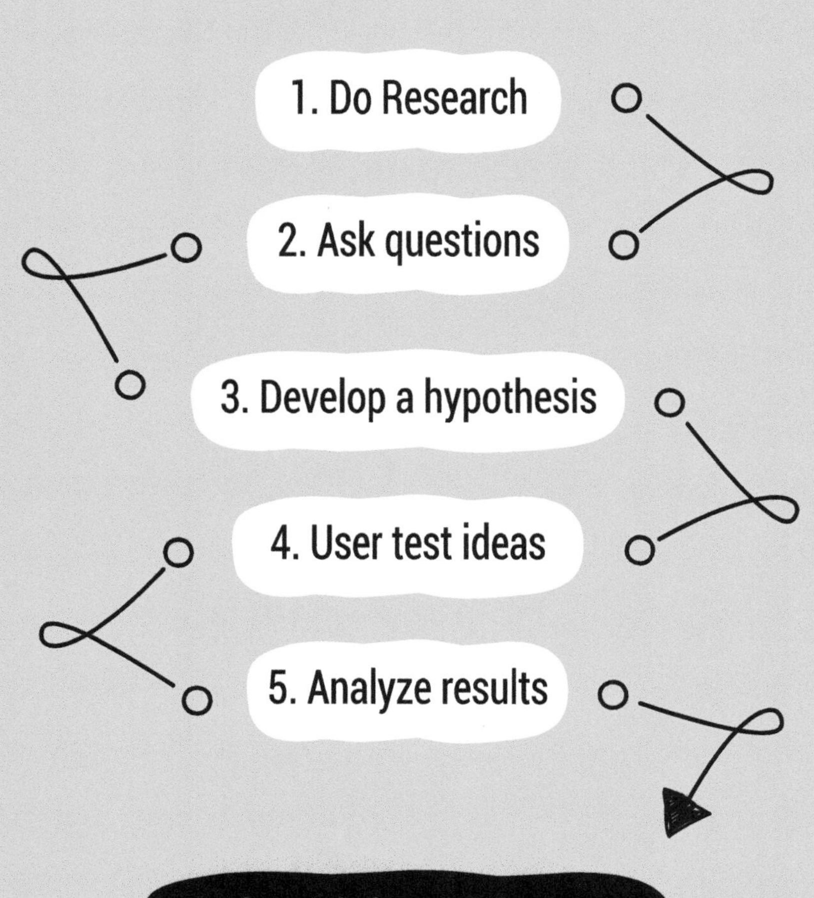

DON'T MAKE DECISIONS BASED ON ASSUMPTIONS

A very important characteristic of User Experience Design is trying to avoid educated guesses as much as possible and this is very much connected to how UX Design is probably the least egocentric design form. Making choices based on data and testing your hypothesis is the right way to move forward in a project. Every time user tests show that the initial hypothesis is wrong, UX Designers are actually happy about it. It means that new data was gathered and the product can be further improved.

Instead of educated guesses, you should research the problem, analyze and develop a hypothesis based on what information you found. Always test your ideas and validate the results at the end! This will result in an informed decision and will reduce the chance of errors that could hurt the user, respectively the product.

Innovation means things are getting better.

But each innovation requires new User Experience

UX WILL ALWAYS BE RELEVANT

Am I too late? Is there anything else to learn about people and their pains? Any new challenges to solve? It feels like everything is polished to the maximum and there's no place for improvement, but of course this is not true at all!

The truth is no digital project is ever finished! Digital products are always changing, shifting in sync with people's constant desire for improvement. Is Facebook ever finished after hitting two billion users? Or Amazon after securing their clear monopole over online shopping? Of course not, all products need to be up to date with the latest standards of accessibility, security or technology, just to name a few crucial aspects.

Technology evolves in an unimaginably fast way and that means a User Experience Designer will never be out of challenges.

RULES
&METHODS

IN **UX DESIGN**

UX Design
EXPLAINED

CONTENT

WHAT WE WANT
TO PRESENT

USER
INTERFACE

HOW WE WANT
TO PRESENT IT

USER
EXPERIENCE

WHAT'S THE EXPERIENCE
WE ARE LOOKING FOR

THE PLACE OF UX DESIGN IN OUR PRODUCTS

Two things can happen after this page. You can either have an uncontrollable urge to find the closest place that sells fruit cakes or you might have an EUREKA! moment about the place of UX Design when looking at a project from a bird's eye view. But my hope is that one does not exclude the other.

A relevant analogy to make is that people don't want to buy four wheels and a shift gear. They want to buy a convenient way of transportation instead, that is always accessible. This is what UX Design works with, the experience of the people interacting with a product.
Not how a product looks, but how it feels.

In this chapter we will look at the most frequent methods of the industry that every UX Designer should know about and see when and why each are used.

UX Methods
COMPARED

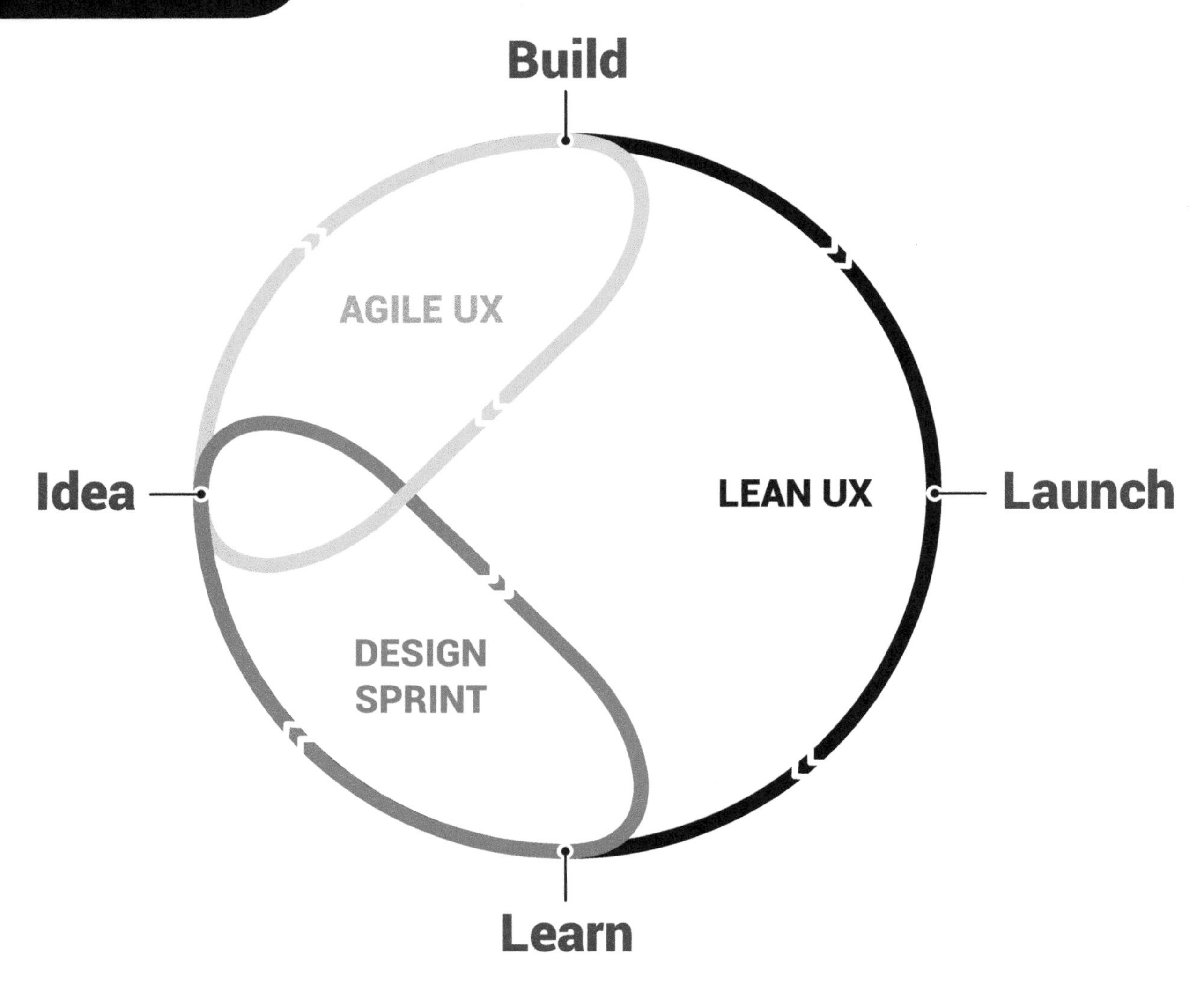

BREAKING DOWN METHODS OF UX DESIGN

In an efficient UX Design process, the whole team follows the same method and workflow. We are going to talk about the most frequently applied methods in UX Design that every designer should learn. You will definitely meet with each of these three methods in your career because they are globally wide-spread.

Looking at the main circle you can recognize the four main steps of the process we discussed earlier, but the terminology is slightly different.
This is what we call the Lean UX process.

You can also observe the iterative nature of UX Design. You can always come back to the previous step, depending on which process you are following.

It's also important to learn that all these methods can be simultaneously applied and each has its distinctive advantage. Let's dive into each!

Agile UX

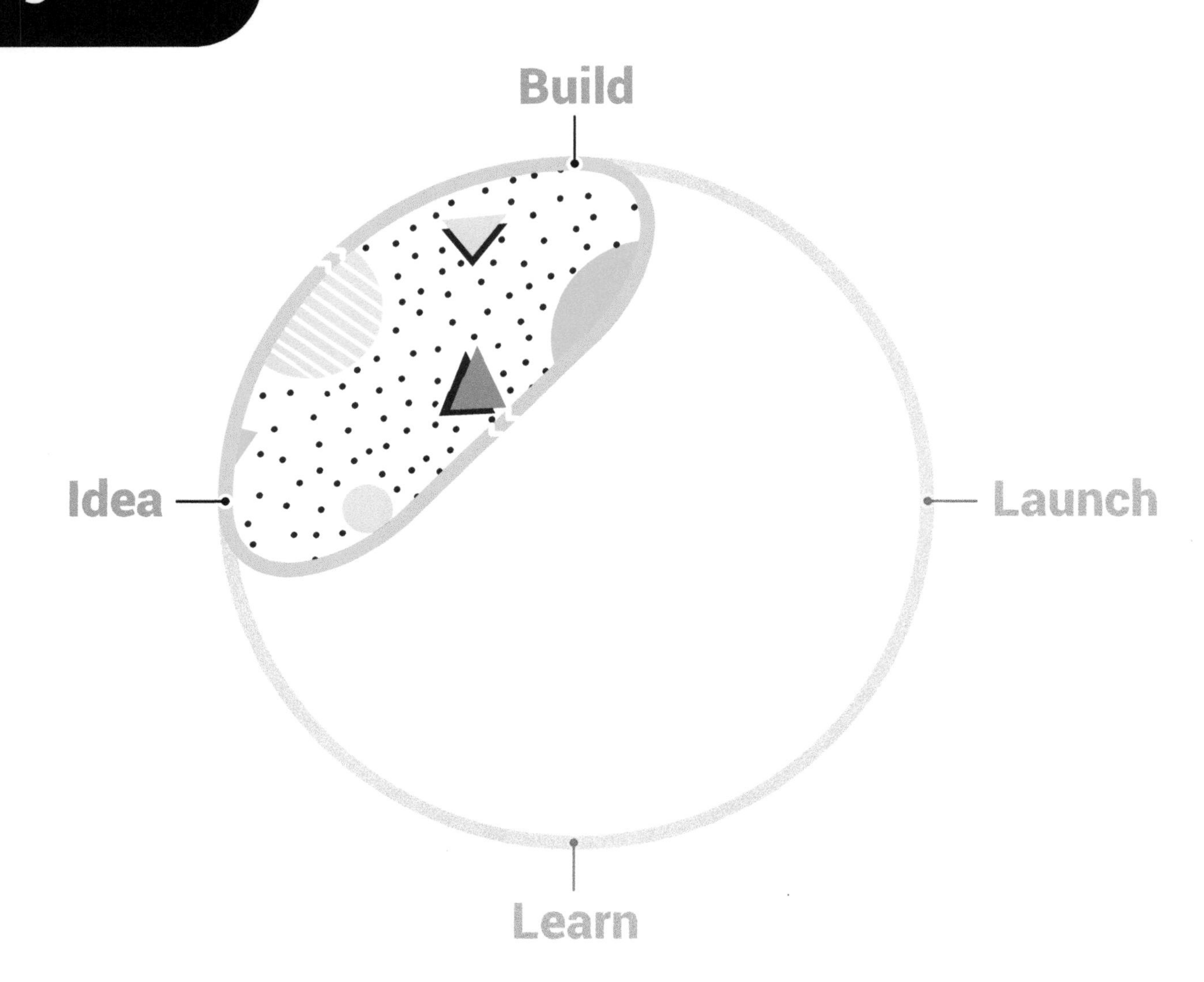

UX METHOD:
AGILE UX

The whole process of product development is called a Lean process and it goes through four phases: Learn, Ideate, Build and Launch. Yes, naturally every UX process ends with launching a new product or feature. But very often iterations happen along the way and one method of iteration is working in an Agile environment.

The agile environment is a loop like fast process that helps teams remain connected and it encourages adjustments to fit the organization's current needs.

Most often the sprint of the design team comes before the sprint of the development team. The design team needs to be at least one step ahead of development so the latter is always ready to start working on new iterations.

The agile methodology is a very collaborative workflow where every department has a seat at the table and decisions take count of everyone's opinion and estimation.

Agile UX WORKFLOW

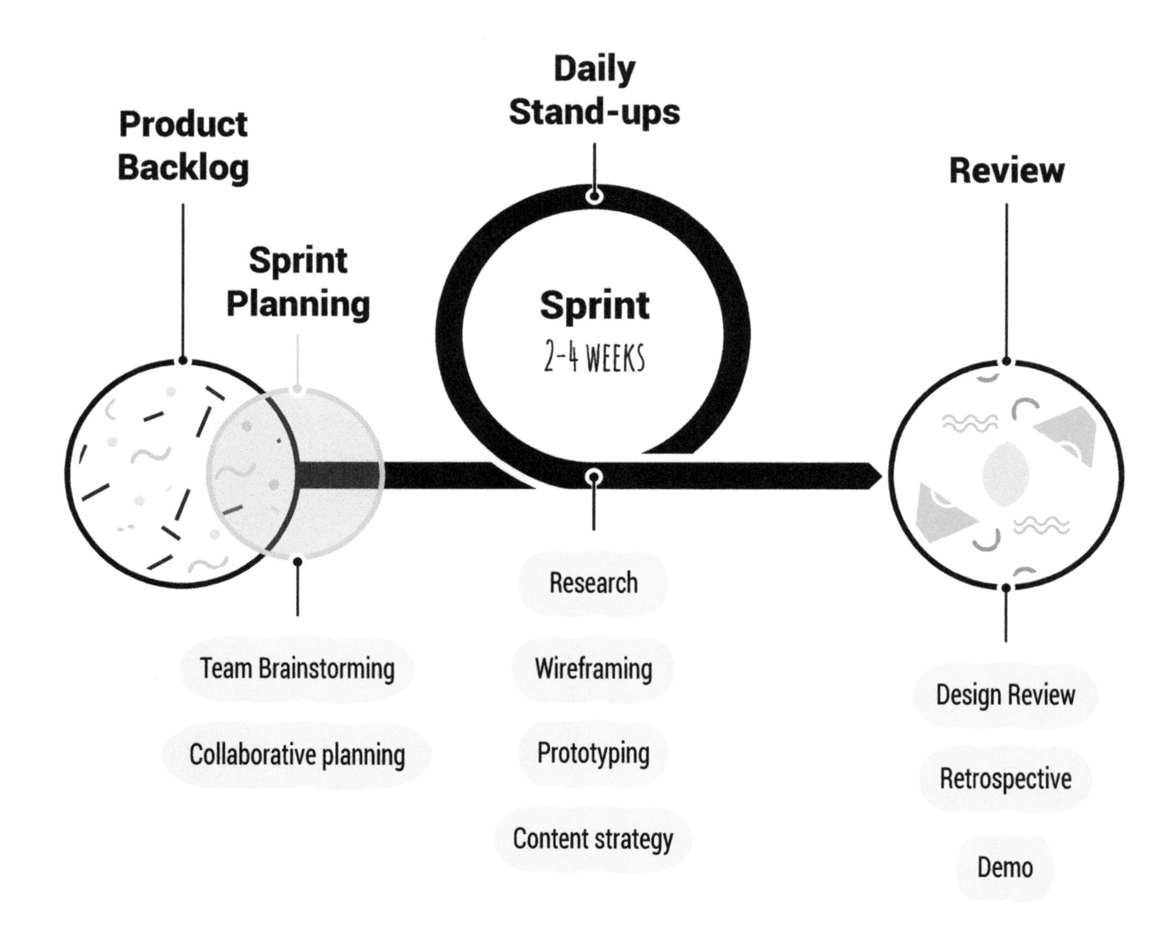

THE AGILE UX WORKFLOW

Most often the Agile workflow is implemented in sprints, usually a two to four weeks period where the whole team has incremental focuses and they communicate through daily standups. Fun fact, it's called a standup because meetings were actually held standing up, so they didn't take too long.

The scope of an upcoming sprint can always change and new priorities can appear. An Agile process works with a product backlog which is basically a wishlist of all the features the team would like to build somewhere in the future. In the beginning of a sprint, the team decides together what features will be selected for development.

There is a big difference between Lean and Agile mentality. In the Lean process you build, launch and iterate based on real user's feedback. In the Agile process there's more revision before launching, which results in a more complete product, not a minimum viable product.

Design Sprint

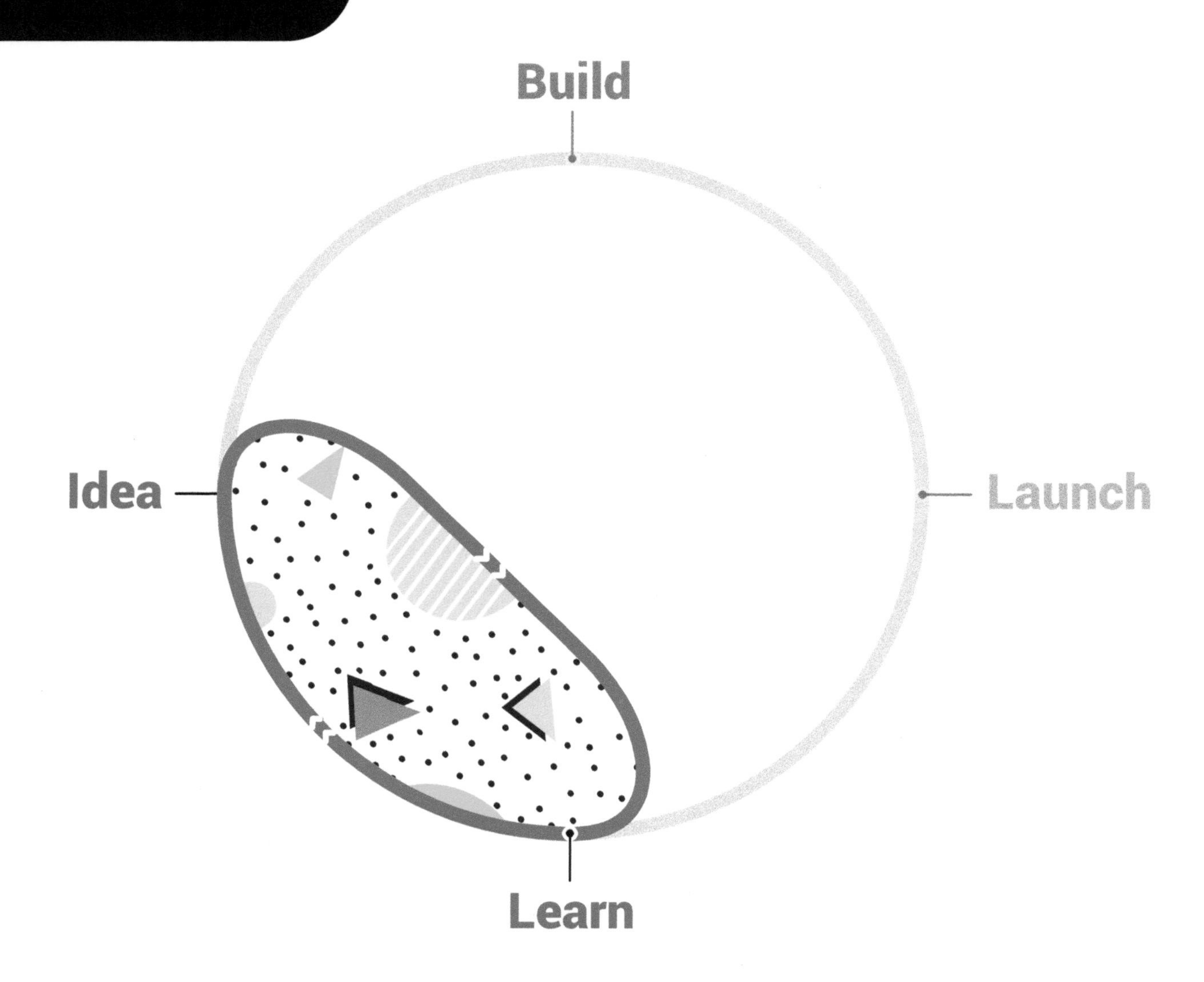

UX METHOD: DESIGN SPRINT

The Design sprint is a fairly new method, compared to the Agile and Lean methodologies, but it's very powerful and ever growing in popularity. It's invented by Jake Knapp while he was working at Google. You can check out his book called "Sprint, Solve big problems and test new ideas in just five days". The book title is probably the best explanation of what a Design Sprint is.

Design sprint is used only at the beginning of a new project or feature development because its purpose is to validate the idea before investing a lot of intellectual and financial resources. This is the key selling point of Design Sprints, as it helps to avoid building faulty ideas and investing only in features with great potential.

Not to mention, it's five days of fun exercises where the whole client team feels involved and therefore invested in the decisions that were taken.

Design Sprint WORKFLOW

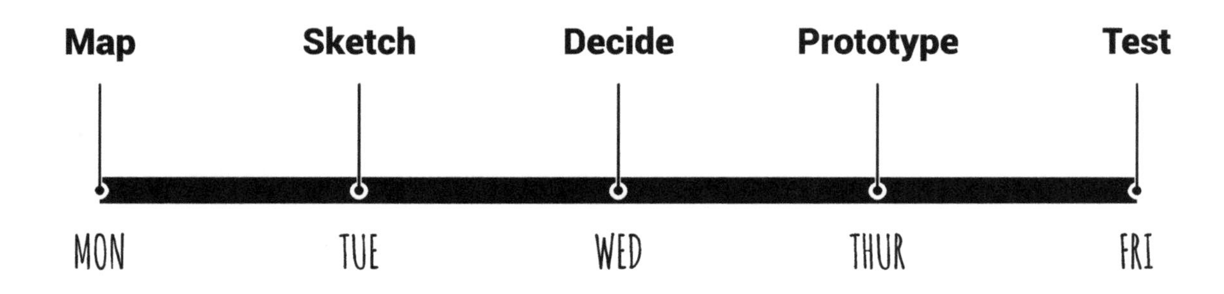

MON

- Assumptions
- Questions

- Ask experts

- Map the flow
- HMW notes
- Pick a target

TUE

- Lightning demo
- Capture ideas

Individual

- Create notes
- ideas
- Crazy 8
- Concept

WED

- Sticky Decision

Individual

- Group discussion

Decider

- Makes the call
- Rumble
- Storyboard

THUR

- Realistic mock
- Divide storyboard
- Define jobs

- Trial Run
- Final touches

FRI

- 1on1 interviews
- Show prototype
- Watch reactions
- Take notes
- Look back
- Answer assumptions
- Draw conclusion

DESIGN SPRINT:
A 5-DAY PROCESS

Initially it was a five-day process, although since the Jake Knapp's book appeared it was further simplified into a four day exercise.
Both versions contain the same exercises, so let's focus on the one you will most probably meet with in your design journey. The five day process.

The design sprint's purpose is to come up with great ideas that in the fifth day can also be validated. It should involve a facilitator, stakeholders, key members of the team from different departments and a designer who will create quick prototypes for the fifth day when the ideas will be tested by potential end users.

I would suggest to dig deep into each exercise of every day presented on the left because Designs Sprints will become more and more a necessity in the future.

It's important to mention that Design Sprints work best in person and it would be hard to implement it online!

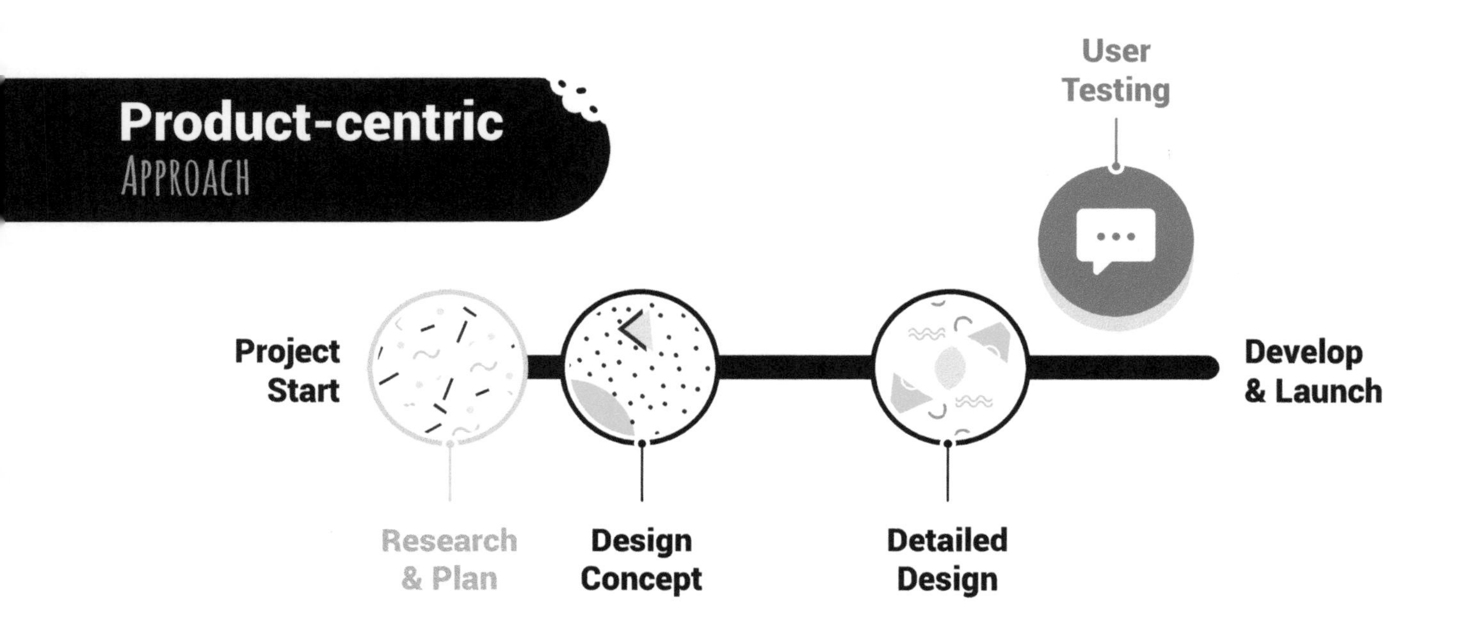
Product-centric
Approach
User
Testing
Project
Start
Develop
& Launch
Research
& Plan
Design
Concept
Detailed
Design

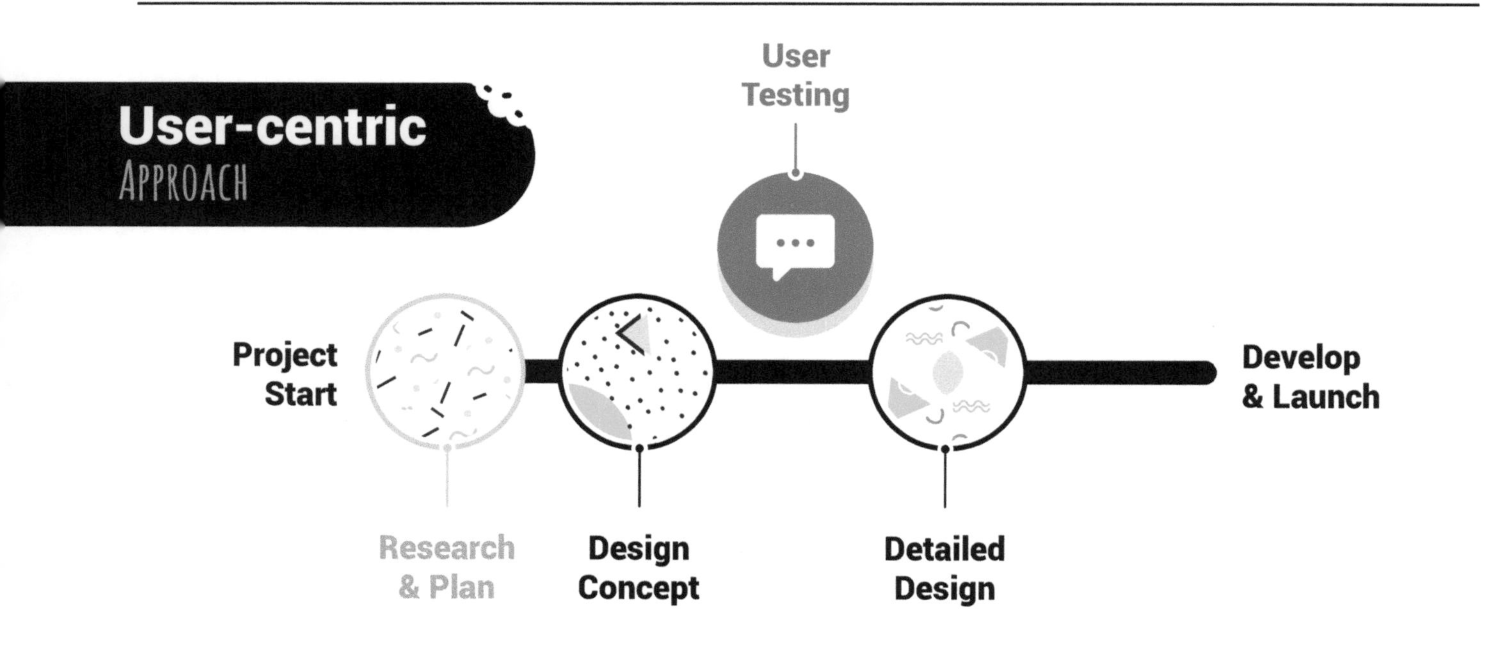
User
Testing
User-centric
Approach
Project
Start
Develop
& Launch
Research
& Plan
Design
Concept
Detailed
Design

A GOOD UX DESIGN IS USER-CENTRIC

Even before the term User Experience Designer existed, User-Centric Design started to gain popularity as an important shift from Product-Centric design.

More and more designers, but especially Don Norman, who conceptualized the term, started to realize the importance of designing with the user in mind, instead of focusing on technologically great features that the users might have never wanted in the first place. Don Norman was working at Apple at the time when he realized that a great experience starts right from the store, followed by the moment the customer takes the product out from the box, and not just while using it.

This switch to being User-Centric meant that the end user needed to be involved more and more and here on the left you can see how actually a small change of order in the process can ultimately create a better product.

User-Centric design was the first crucial change in direction to making research a core part of UX Design.

THIS IS A
Design System

BUTTON

TEXT FIELD

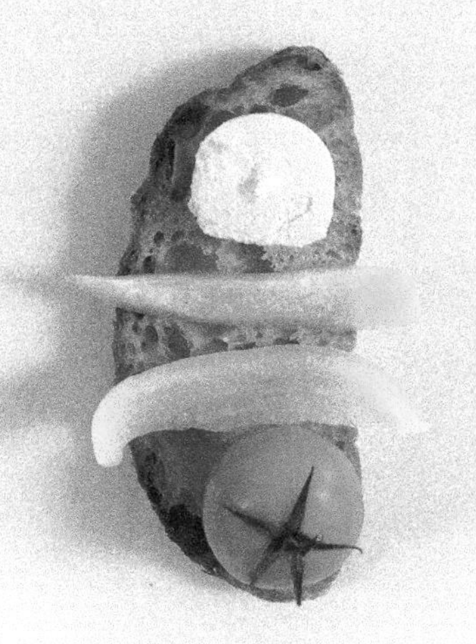

LOGIN PAGE

WHAT IS A DESIGN SYSTEM AND WHY SHOULD YOU CARE?

In the recent years, the term Design System hit the product design community as a great phenomenon that will give an equal fighting power to small startups and large enterprises.

Design systems are essentially a collection of rules and principles that work as templates for every new element or page that the product needs.

A design system contains style guides, but it's much more than that! It contains all the fonts, logos, brand colors and attributes.

The smallest unit in a design system is called an atom and more atoms form a component.
A button, for example, is a component built from the shape and the text of the button, which are both atoms. When you create a new page, you use all the components like buttons, fields, paragraphs, headlines and so on. This kind of granulation will help projects easily scale and remain consistent at the same time. It also helps collaborative work because anyone who would start working on the project, could follow the same rules.

UNDERSTANDING

THE
USER

I am your user
and this is what I need

THE IMPORTANCE OF UNDERSTANDING THE USER

This book is slowly building on the importance of a user focused approach, which is the essential principle in User Experience Design.

There's a famous saying in the industry that says "you are not your user". This highlights a very simple but powerful truth about the relevance of discovering, observing and understanding your target audience, because they are the ones who will eventually make or brake your product, not your cutting edge interface design, nor the newest technology used.

Fortunately, the needs of the users are universal and can be systematized into just a couple of main aspects, which I will try to present in the next chapter.

Of course, we need to keep in mind that these universal truths must be applied into the specific context of the product, but they work very well as a general starting point and guidance.

I'm in a hurry
toc
tic
toc
tic
toc

1. PEOPLE DON'T HAVE TIME TO FIGURE OUT YOUR DESIGNS

Interviewing your target audience is a very effective method to understand their desires and pains, but you must be cautious! Day-by-day life is usually much busier than your home/work office or coffee shop where you design your screens. This means that what people say in a user interview, which is a relaxed environment, might be very different from what people actually do in their swamped schedule.

People are always in a hurry. This translates into a platform that doesn't hide an important feature under a minimal look. Research reveals what is the primary value that a platform can offer to the user. These values should immediately catch the user's attention and every second spent on understanding them represents a usability issue. Users in a hurry after all, they don't have time to figure out your product!

I'm happy with
my current wheel

2. DESIGN BASED ON USER EXPECTATIONS

As a general rule, user expectations should always be respected, but of course each user has different experience and understanding of how products generally work. That's why research is so crucial to understand your specific target audience's needs, wants and pains. But more about research a bit later, in a dedicated chapter.

The most palpable and easy to understand example for differences in user expectations must be people's way of speaking. Teenagers speak very different compared to let's say elderly people and both should be addressed in a language they can naturally relate to, otherwise neither will feel like they belong.

But User Expectation is about something else too, about not innovating when it's not necessary, because that might hurt your product. If nobody has a problem with the way they navigate on your website, changing that will add an unnecessary learning curve to the product.

Thanks for the encouragement!
GREAT JOB!

3. USERS ARE LOOKING FOR WAYS TO IMPROVE THEIR LIVES

Improve your user's life and they will adopt your platform in no time! Make them a better multitasker, runner, swimmer. Make them more organized, more relaxed or just a bit more informed every day.
People are looking for offers. Cheaper trips, two meals for the price of one and if possible, why not a free massage over the weekend.

Now you most probably can't offer these through your platform without a clear path to bankruptcy, but there are so many ways people's life can be improved. Only think about yours and how many times you are stressed out or just in a hurry. If your life can be improved, than so is everybody else's.

A good exercise would be to take into account the platforms that you use most often and try to realize how they improve your life. There is no successful platform out there that doesn't offer any benefit to the user and you should thrive for that too!

Be honest with me!
100%

4. BUILDING TRUST IS ESSENTIAL

This is a little secret from me because you were super nice to buy this book. By the way, I hope you are happy with it so far! Here it is: people are already coming to your platform with skepticism. Are you any good or just a waste of time? Do you actually offer what you promised on your marketing page? I am your user and I'm here to find out. But waste my time and I will never come back here, I promise you that!

This analogy translates into the ethical approach of being always honest with your users. I'm sure all of you have met this scenario: if you tell your users that there's only one room left, that should be true; if you tell your users that a product will cost two bucks, it shouldn't be three bucks in the end.

You look familiar!

5. PEOPLE UNDERSTAND WHAT'S FAMILIAR

Jakob Nielsen is one of the pioneers of User Experience Design who, together with Don Norman, conceptualized and formed the early ages of UX, and they are shaping it since.

Jabok Nielsen created a guide of ten general principles to follow in design. These are called the ten heuristics.

One of the ten heuristics is how people spend most of their times on other websites. This means that they expect that your site (or app) works the same way as the neighbour's platform.

Sorry, don't care how,
just make it work

6. PEOPLE CARE ONLY ABOUT SOLVING THEIR PROBLEM

You worked on your project for months, you know it like the back of your palm and naturally you are very invested in every molecule of it. You can answer any question about it if someone wakes you up in the middle of the night, like it's a math test you prepared for ages. This also means that every shortcut to each solution could seem obvious to you, but in fact the user's perspective couldn't be more different from yours.

You might have gone to great lengths to solve an issue that came up, but the user will only care if it's working or not. You might have worked on a feature for months to polish it to the max, but the user will abandon it the second someone is doing a better job than you.

Be redundant and explanatory to the extremes with the actions a user can take in your interface. Treat users like they are at their first visit in your platform, so they don't need to base their experience on memory.

IF A PRODUCT
NEEDS A MANUAL,
IT'S BROKEN!

GREAT PRODUCTS DON'T COME WITH A MANUAL

The biggest shift from product-centric to user-centric design meant that we gave up on the idea that users should learn how to use a tool in order to handle it. Now this is still true in cases of professional tools, I'm not suggesting that airplane pilots shouldn't go through rigorous training.

But when it comes to customer products, a manual is the first sign of a faulty product. This philosophy influenced a great deal the adoption of apps, imagine a world where the new Gmail app would come with instructions!

We associate this manual-less world with an easy learning curve for the user. This translates into the amount of time a user needs to figure out how to handle a product.
Of course, the fastest, the better!

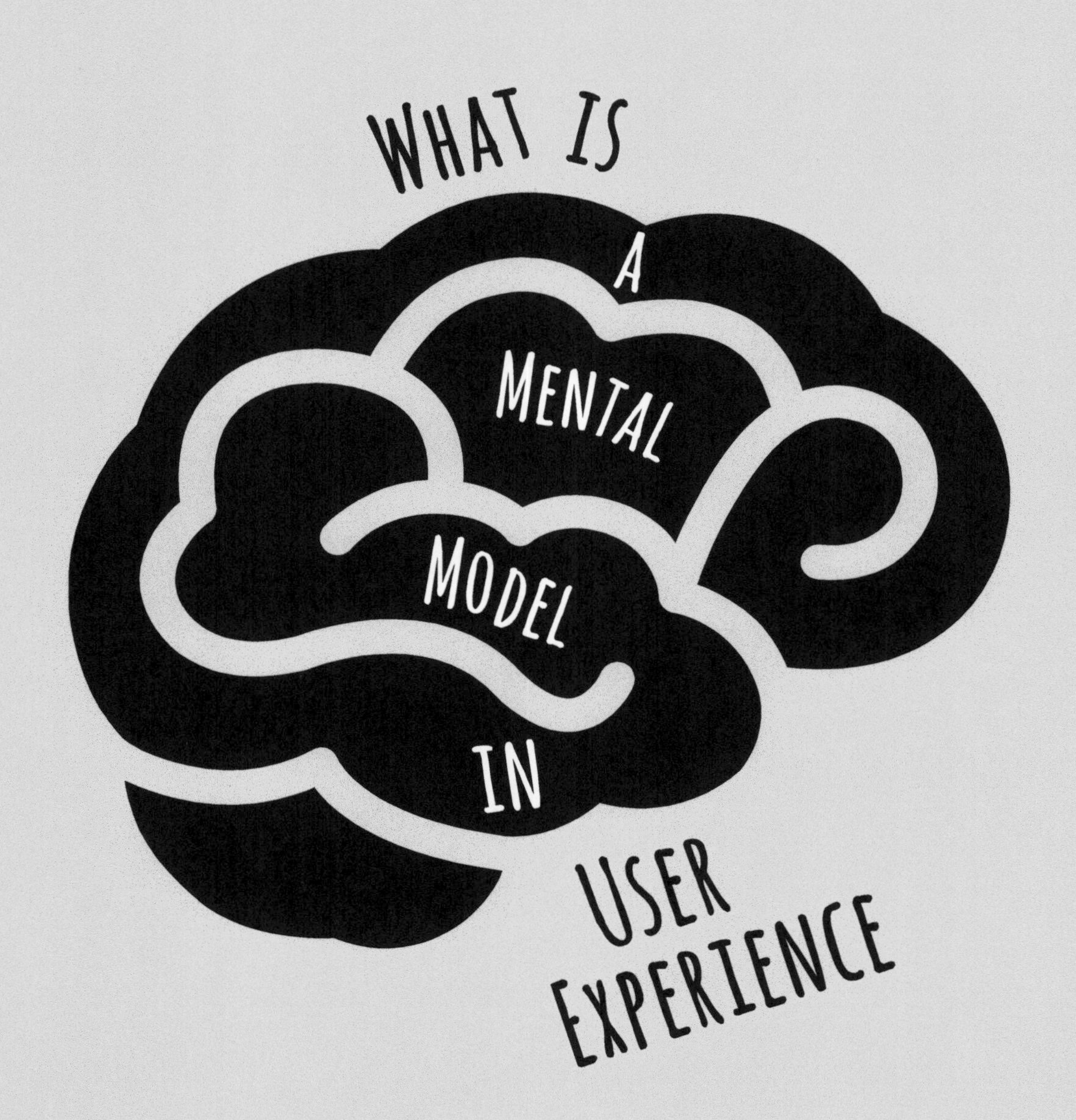
WHAT IS
A
MENTAL
MODEL
IN
USER
EXPERIENCE

UNDERSTANDING PEOPLE'S MENTAL MODELS

Let's define Mental Models so we can quickly make this term friendlier. I know from my experience that hearing about Mental Models the first time was quite overwhelming.

It's actually very simple: Mental Models are people's expectations of how something should work, based on their past experiences. For example, If people use 100 e-shops that places an "add to cart" button at the top right corner of the screen, that is where they will expect it to be in in the 101th e-shop too.

Sometimes designers find it hard to respect people's mental models because they are not based on facts but on their personal experiences and beliefs, but this mistake can easily break a product. For example, once Chrysler reimagined the gear shift, even if it might have been a super design, it behaved too different for the drivers, so they had to call back 1 million cars just to make changes on the gear shift's design.

Jakob's Law

Users spend most of their time on other sites

Users prefer your site to work
the same way as all the other sites
they already know

JAKOB NIELSEN'S LAW OF FAMILIARITY

I hope this chapter offered a little clarity and hopefully made the desire to understand the target audience a much more approachable idea.

I mentioned already the influence of Jakob Nielsen in the UX field and I will continue to encourage to dive deep in all his extensive contribution together with Don Norman. His 10 Heuristics of Interaction design remains a crucial information to consume.

One of the Heuristics is about how the user is looking for familiarity. They spend 90% of their time on other platforms. When they come to yours, they expect it to work the same. This rule of thumb emphasizes the relevance of mental models.

We know what we need to learn about our users, but the question "how" remains unanswered. In the next chapter we will discuss in detail the most frequent research methods that will help you gather the right data and use it the right way!

USER EXPERIENCE

RESEARCH METHODS

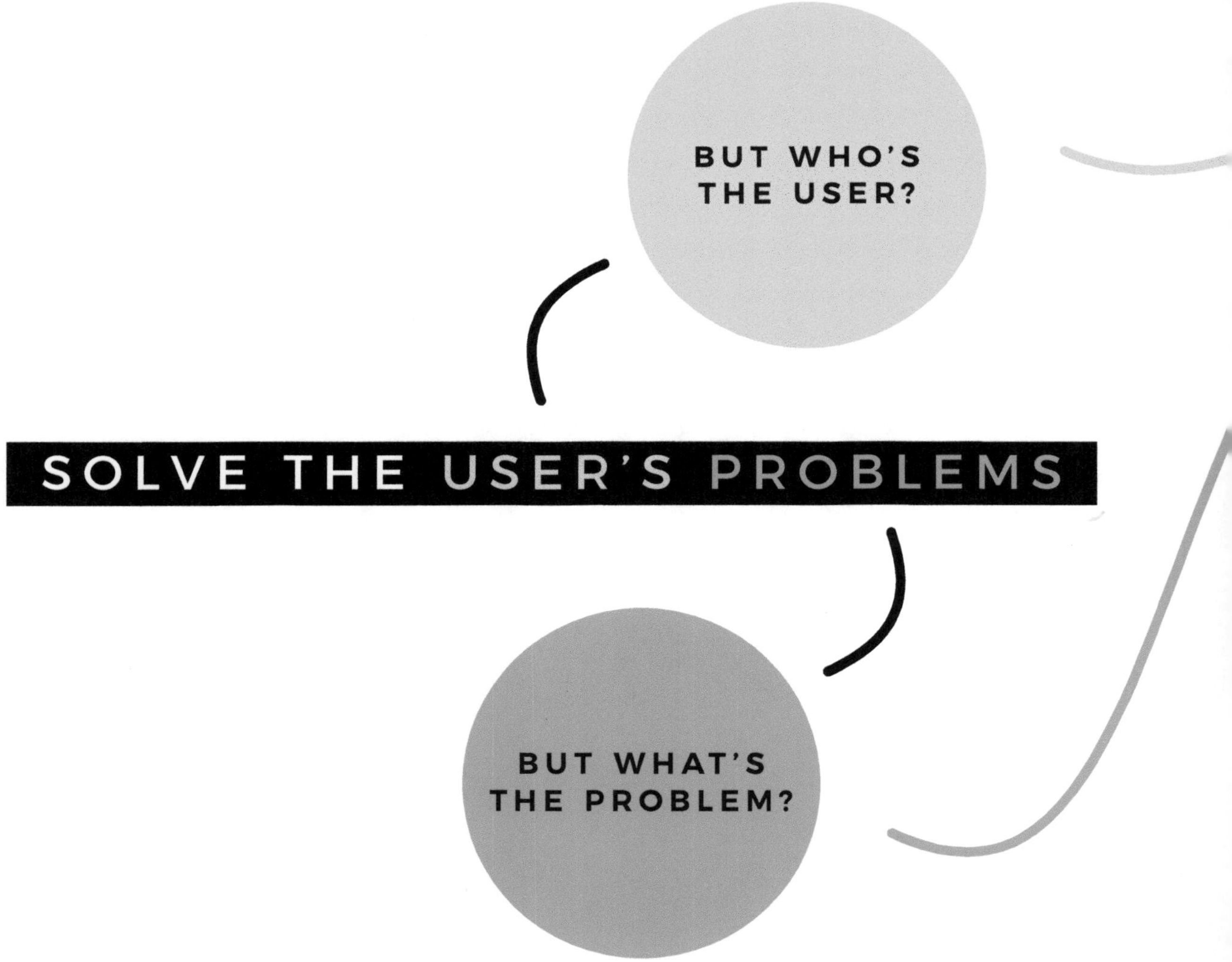

SOLVE THE USER'S PROBLEMS

BUT WHO'S THE USER?

BUT WHAT'S THE PROBLEM?

UX RESEARCH IS VITAL TO UNDERSTAND THE USER

UX Research is the first step of a healthy UX Process and it's vital to understand the user you are designing for. Research, in my experience, is often the most ignored factor of the design process, which usually leads to faulty assumptions and inevitably a failed product that users won't adopt.

UX Design is a method to solve the user's problem. But who's the user? And what's the problem? These questions can be answered only with research and we will learn how in the following pages.

You probably think about lab coats, chemicals and protective glasses every time you hear the word research, it can be scary at first. My hope is that after the end of this chapter you will consider it approachable, and who knows, maybe even exciting, to start your design process with research as the first step.

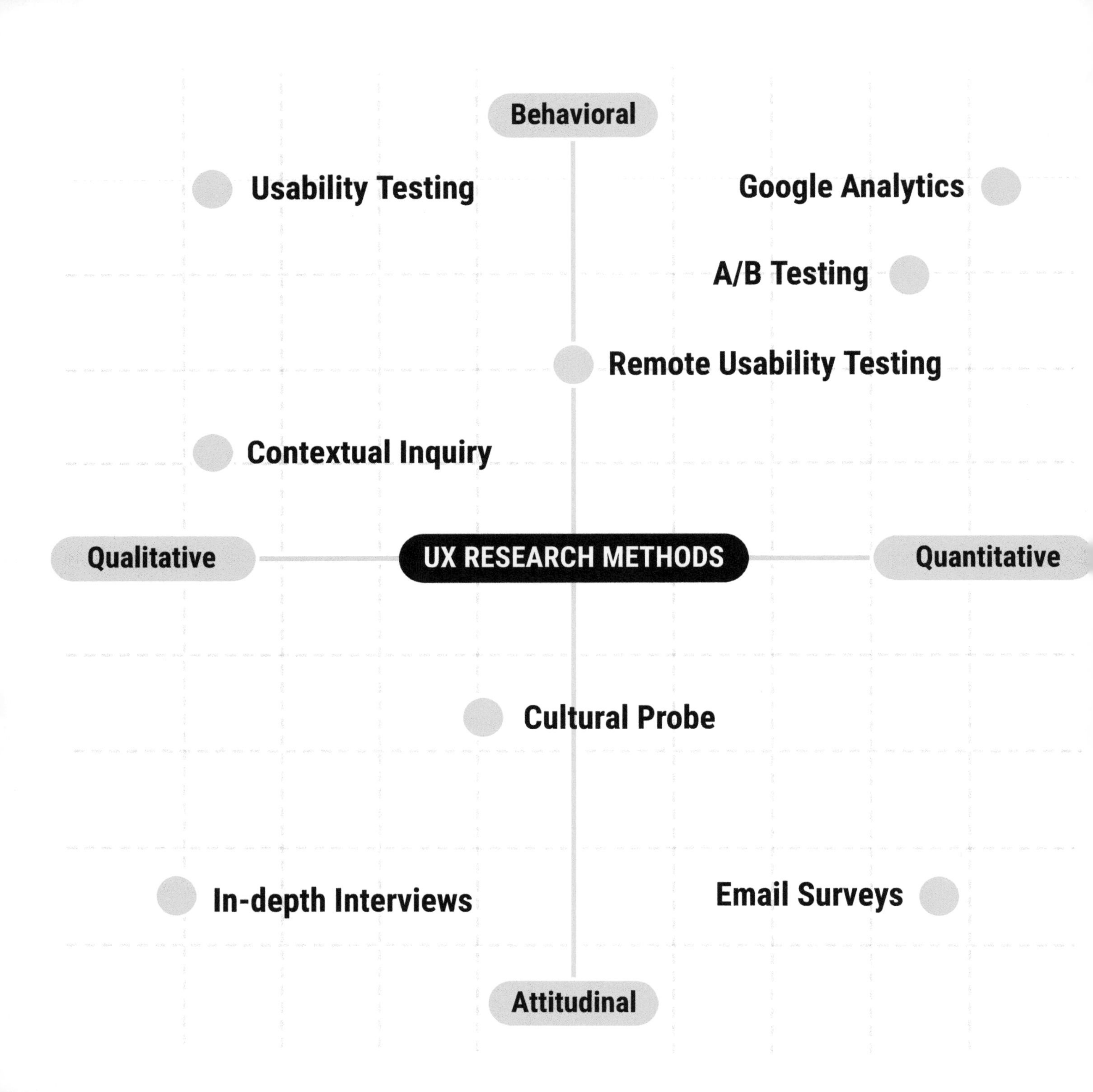
Behavioral
Usability Testing
Google Analytics
A/B Testing
Remote Usability Testing
Contextual Inquiry
Qualitative
UX RESEARCH METHODS
Quantitative
Cultural Probe
In-depth Interviews
Email Surveys
Attitudinal

THE MAP OF ALL UX RESEARCH METHODS

We will deal with each research and testing method in detail, but it's important to start to place them on the same canvas first. This should help to understand when to use which method.

All research methods can be placed in two distinctive categories. They are either qualitative or quantitative. Quantitative research is close ended and it answers the question "what". Qualitative research is open ended and it answers the question "why". We will detail both as we move along.

Research can also be attitudinal and behavioral. Attitudinal research focuses on what the user thinks about a certain aspect when behavioral research observes the user's actions in his natural environment. The distinction is relevant because often times users say one thing and do another. So taking the learnings of a user interview with a grain of salt is a good, cautionary idea.

It's time to take each method separately and understand why they are beneficial!

The most frequently used

UX RESEARCH METHODS

Phase	Method	Description
Discover	**Field Study**	Observing people in their natural environment either by a researcher or by Diary Study
Discover	**User Interviews**	Interview with one or multiple people (focus groups), to learn about their perception
Discover	**Stakeholder interviews**	Understand what the stakeholders want to achieve
Define	**User Persona**	Gather demographic and psychographics data about your target, in one place
Define	**Card Sorting**	Helps to define the information architecture of navigation or product categories
Define	**User Journey maps**	Analysing every step of the user around the product, to define their pain points
Define	**User Stories / Jobs to be done**	Both shows the motivations and desires of the user behind the decisions they make
Validate	**Usability Tests**	Validating designs, seeing if the target user finds everything useful and understandable.
Validate	**Analytics review**	Analyzing user data, like heatmaps or analytics to find usability issues
Validate	**Surveys**	Surveys for the user to find out more about their experience. Like NPR scores

WHEN TO USE WHICH UX RESEARCH METHOD

There are so many research methods that it can easily become overwhelming to understand when to apply each and why, so it's better to separate them into categories based on the phase the project is in. This way you will need to concentrate only on a few, depending on where you are in the process.

Research methods can be categorized into groups of Discovery and Define and it's important to know that both are applied before working on the actual interface. It's an meaningful observation because it represents the nature of UX Design so well. It shows how data and empathy driven this domain can be.

Only after discovering the user and defining their pain points we can start to work on design. After our mockups are ready, it's time to validate our results with usability tests, various analytic tools, A/B testing or surveys.

Analyze the table on the left to understand when to use which research method. But don't worry, we will learn in detail about each!

5 Users

Is all you need
for a successful
user testing

IS UX RESEARCH COMPLICATED? NOT AT ALL!

Before we dig deep into each research method separately, I would like to highlight the fact that the gain is so much higher than the pain when it comes to research.

You decided which research method you should apply, but where do you find hundreds of right users to apply it to? I would like to eliminate this problem early in this chapter because actually for most research you don't need more than five users. Research shows that five users can reveal 80% of the usability issues and it starts to repeat after that. So it's better to do small incremental tests with five users, solve the issues you've found and then test again.

It's important to mention that this rule works only for qualitative usability testing, not for quantitative research like A/B testing, where you need to test with as many users as possible.

Quantitative
research

vs

Qualitative
research

Which fruit
is your favorite?

OR

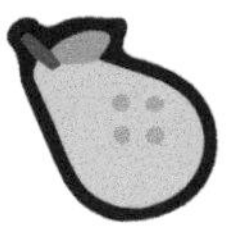

Tell me about
your favorite fruit

Collect Numbers
& Metrics

Collect Stories,
Experience

3.SET UP THE VARIABLES

Test only one thing at a time.
For example should a button say
Sign up or **Register** or **Submit**

4.BE PATIENT

Wait at least a week (if not a month)
to have a valid result.

You can use abtasty.com to calculate how many users you need for your test

while you can conduct a great research with few people, A/B testing and analytics need as many data as possible for an accurate result.

CARD SORTING TECHNIQUE

Sounds like a game and I actually consider it very close to one, because it's such a fun exercise for defining a site's or app's information architecture. But it doesn't only exist for the sake of playing a game. It's an efficient way to define your platform's navigation in a way that it makes sense for the target audience. For example, if you have an online shop, you need to find a way to organize all your items, and card sorting is just the tool for that!

There are 2 types of card sorting. Open-ended, when testers order the cards without any predefined groups, and close-ended, when testers order the cards into groups already predefined. I'll detail on the next page how to conduct open-ended card sorting in just three steps.

You could try out card sorting with famous platforms, for fun. Take instagram for example and apply these three steps, see what happens! And while you're there, look up @uxbites to say hi! Everyone who discovers this easter egg receives a piece of chocolate!

HOW TO DO CARD SORTING

STEP 1:

Let's say you are doing card sorting for an e-commerce site: Write down all the categories you want to organize onto cards.

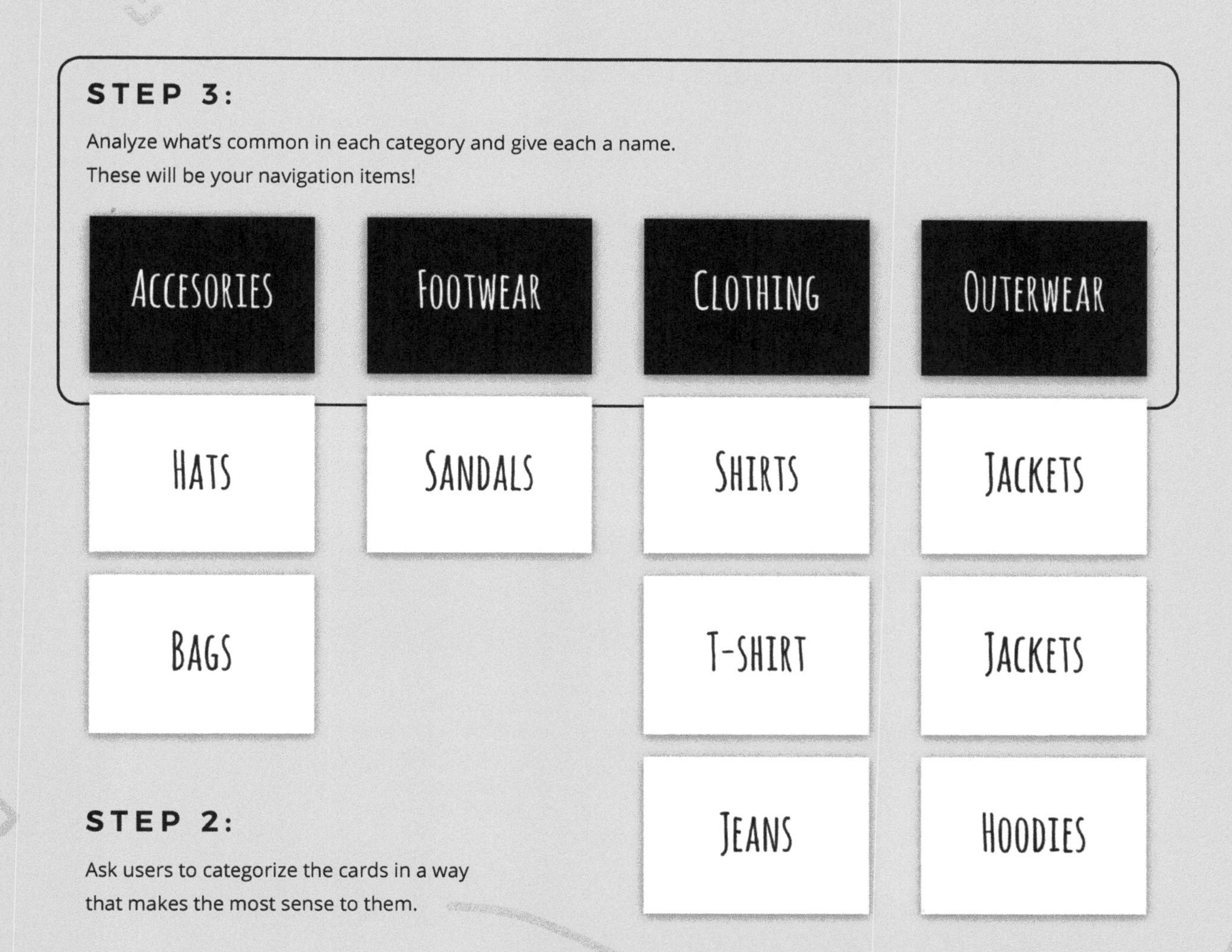
STEP 3:
Analyze what's common in each category and give each a name.
These will be your navigation items!
ACCESORIES
FOOTWEAR
CLOTHING
OUTERWEAR
HATS
SANDALS
SHIRTS
JACKETS
BAGS
T-SHIRT
JACKETS
JEANS
HOODIES
STEP 2:
Ask users to categorize the cards in a way
that makes the most sense to them.

QUALITATIVE RESEARCH

USER INTERVIEWS

Probably the easiest research method, it basically means having a conversation with your target. It's one of the most important ones too, especially at the beginning of a project. It reveals information about the user's desires you couldn't have predicted otherwise. Just, as a rule of thumb, take what people say with a grain of salt, because it's usually slightly different from how they actually behave.

FIELD STUDIES

As I said, people usually behave differently from what they tell you, so it's important to also observe how they act in their natural environment. Field studies are visits to places that are related to the product you are working on. For example, if you are designing an app to order coffee, you should visit coffee shops and observe people's behavior while they are not thinking about how to answer your questions.

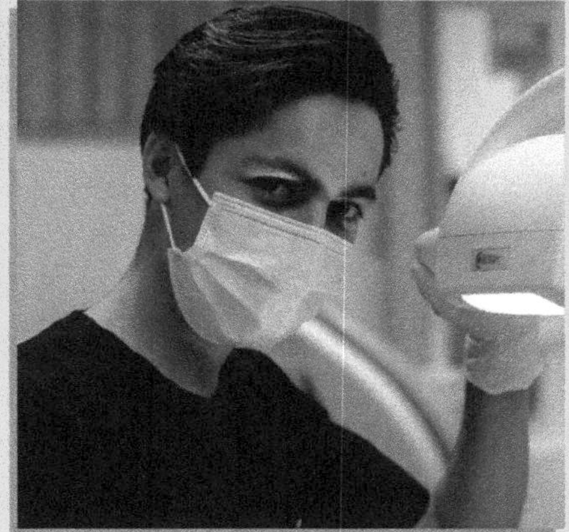

BRAND RESEARCH

COMPETITORS MAP

Researching your users is crucial but it's also imperative to keep the competition in mind. To use this template, pin on these circles all your direct and indirect competition to look out for, study their approach and see how your product differs from theirs.

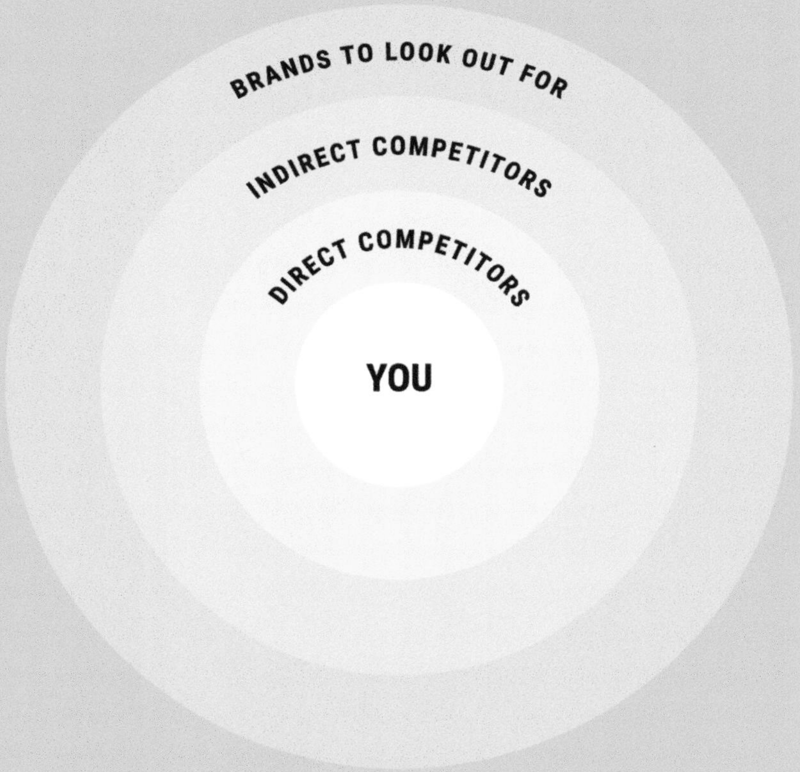

BRANDS TO LOOK OUT FOR

INDIRECT COMPETITORS

DIRECT COMPETITORS

YOU

You can download this template on uxbites.co, for free!

DEFINING THE BRAND'S VOICE

Regarding the brand you are working on, it's necessary to pinpoint the communication style. This might seem important only if you are working in marketing, but it has its significance in UX Writing also. Additionally, you can pin your competition's brand voice on the same map to see what separates you from them.

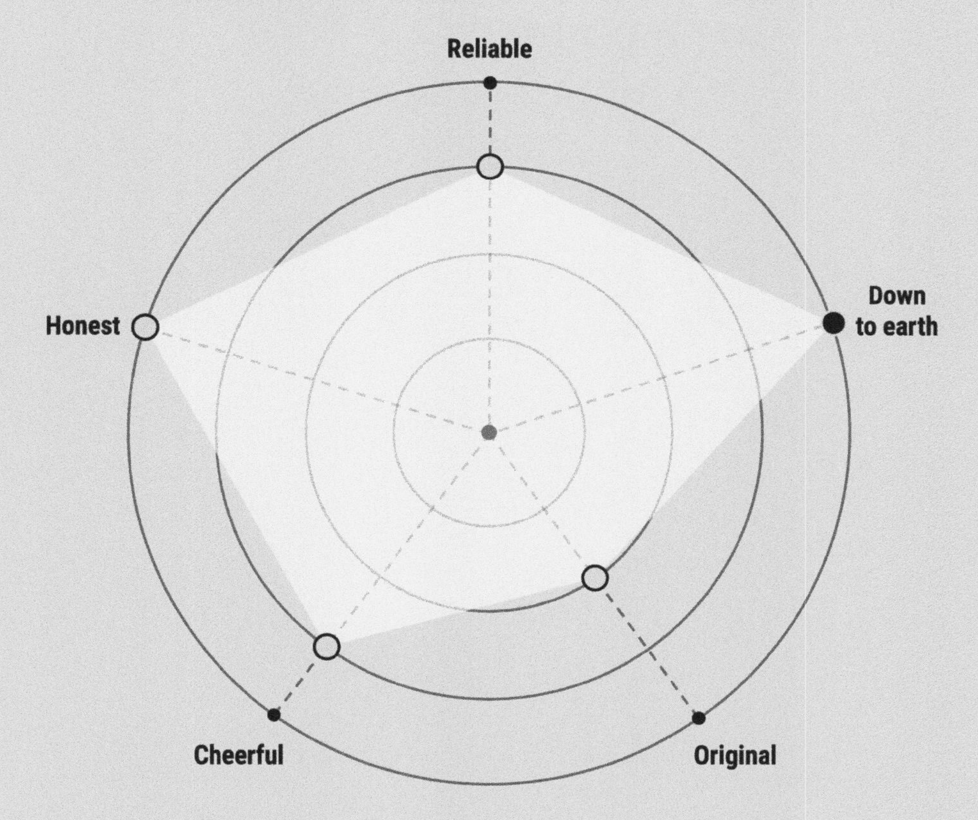

You can download this template on uxbites.co, for free!

How likely are you
to recommend UX Bites
to friends or family?

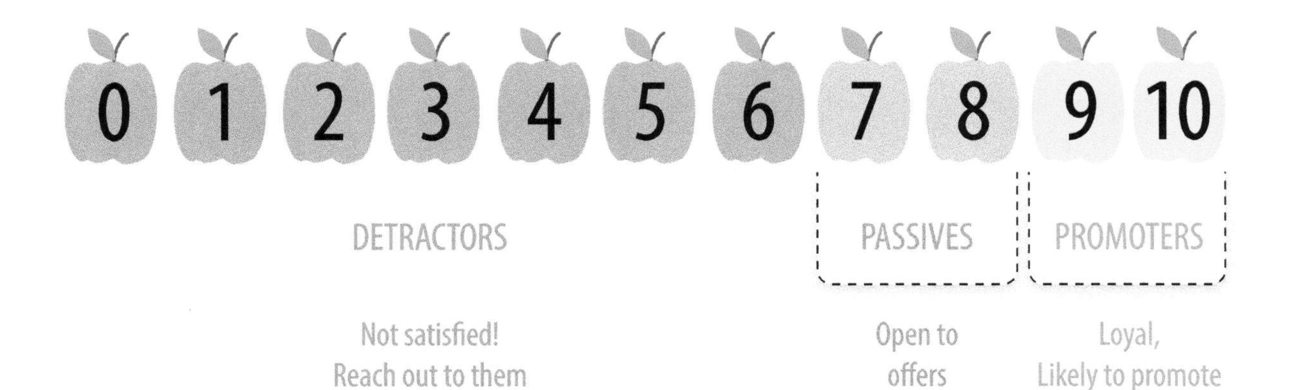

THE NET PROMOTER SCORE: ONE OF THE OLDEST TRICK

What's the most popular and easiest method to measure customer satisfaction? It's nothing new or cutting edge, it's the Net Promoter Score from 2003.

It's a simple question that finds out how likely a user would recommend your product to friends or family. It's also simple for the user to complete the task. They don't need to type anything, there aren't any multiple steps, so it usually brings in very good results.

Did you know? 45% of unsatisfied users take their experience to social media. With NPS you can get ahead of this! Be aware of the users who pick a score between 0 to 6 because they are usually not satisfied. Get in contact with them, try to find out why, to solve the problem before they share it online!

NPS can be used efficiently at big milestones like 90 days in the platform or at the end of a more complex journey, like a checkout process.

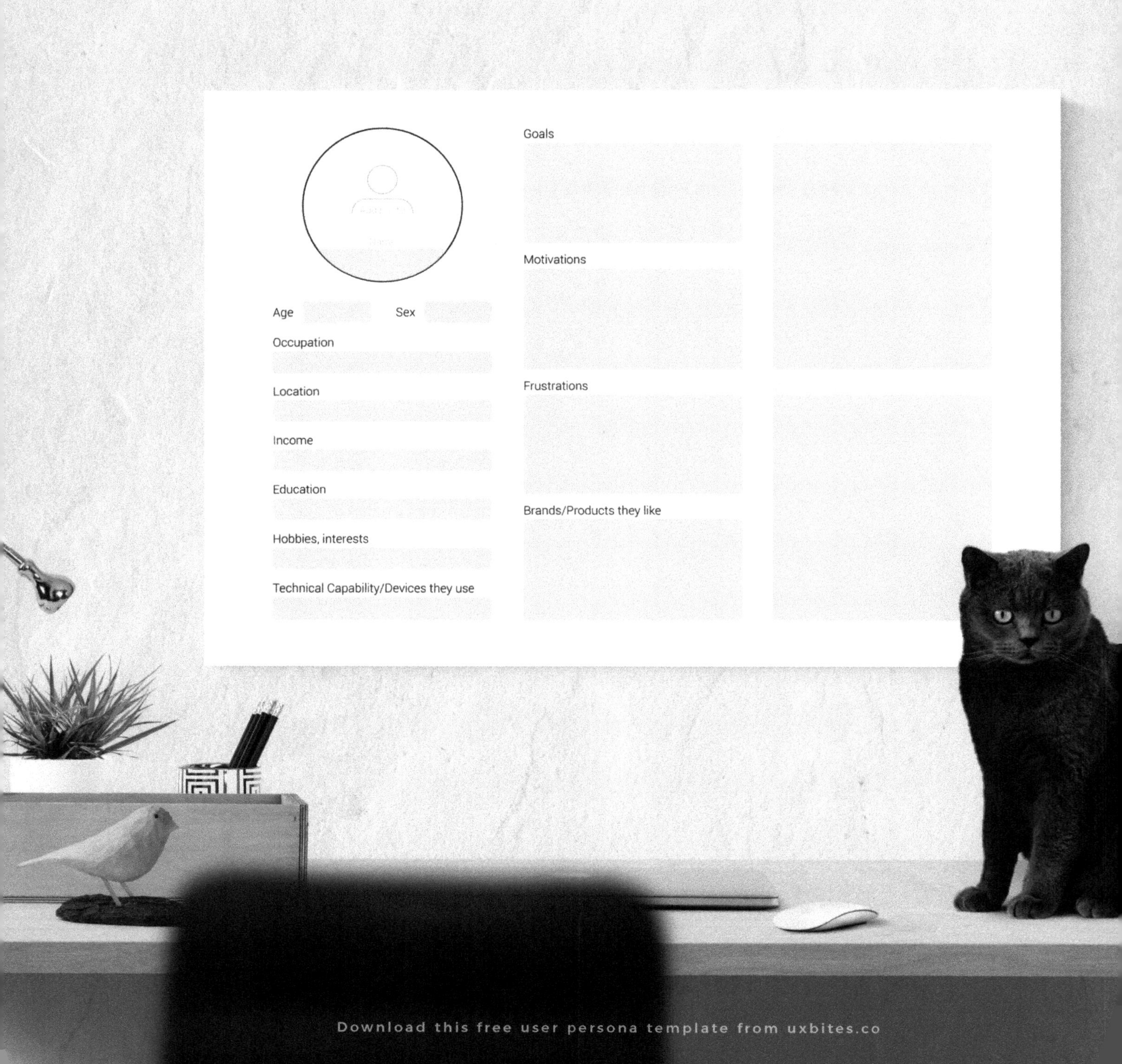
Goals
Motivations
Frustrations
Brands/Products they like
Age
Sex
Occupation
Location
Income
Education
Hobbies, interests
Technical Capability/Devices they use
Download this free user persona template from uxbites.co

TOOLS FOR RESEARCH

THE USER PERSONA TEMPLATE

Doing research means gathering valuable data about your user to better understand how a product can help their everyday life. But the amount of data gathered can be overwhelming sometimes and hard to remember.

In this respect, user persona templates are meant to help you visualize the gathered data. It's like a master directory of everything you've found out about the user. It's a structured view of their demographic data, like their income, occupation, etc. and psychographic data, like their motivations and frustrations.

You can have multiple personas in a project if you have multiple target audiences. For example if you create an app for schools, it will most probably be used by teachers, students and maybe even parents. This means that you would need three separate Personas because their needs can be completely different.

You can download this and other UX Research templates on uxbites.co for free!

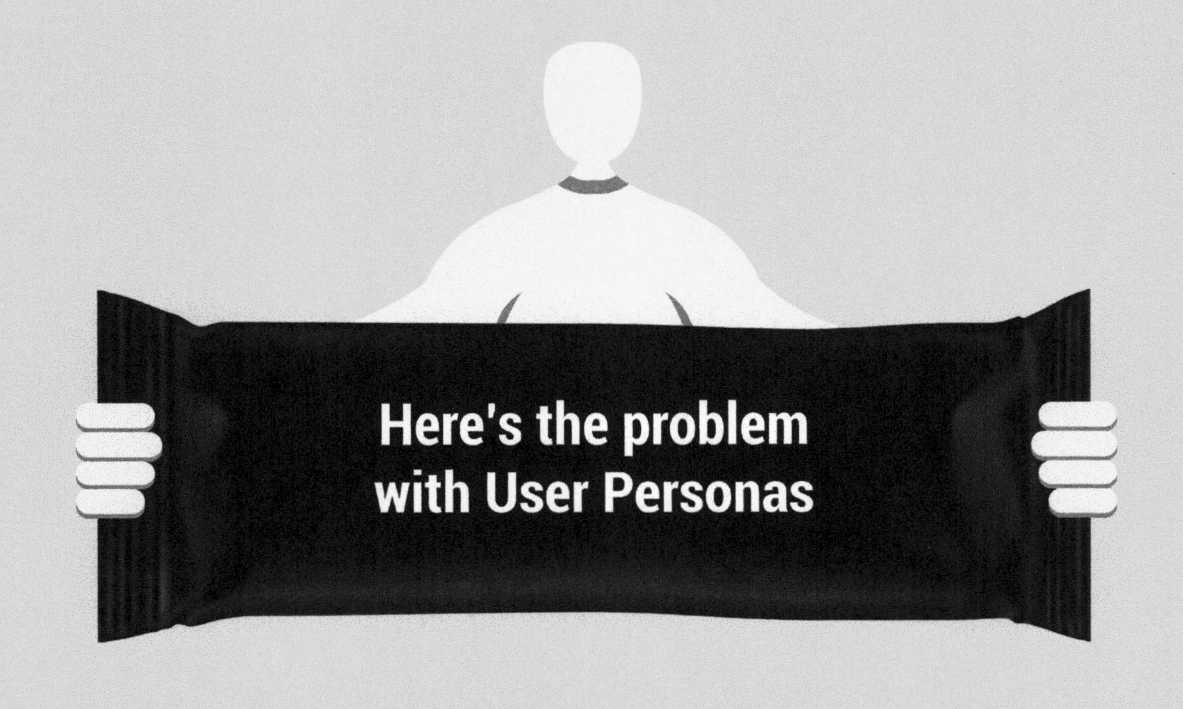

PEOPLE ARE NOT BUYING CHOCOLATE
BECAUSE THEY ARE MALE, 32, AND LIKE MUSIC

BUT BE CAREFUL WITH THE USER PERSONA

While user persona is indispensable, because it helps designers empathize with the user, it's just a template containing the conclusions, not a tool to help you analyze research data. A research type is a method you choose to solve an equation with (learn about your users), while a user persona template is where you gather the result of the equation.

User persona templates are powerful only if they are true. It can be used as a shortcut too, to fill it with information we think we know about the user. A user persona based on assumptions can be a sure path to a product that doesn't serve the user's needs.

While user personas are powerful, I suggest to use them together with the "Jobs to be done", a powerful technique to reveal the user's motivation behind an action, something user personas struggle to visualize. Let's learn "Jobs to be done" with a turn of a page.

THE SITUATION

When

I'M HUNGRY

I HAVE A MEETING

I GO OUTSIDE

THE MOTIVATION

I want to

ORDER FOOD

CALL A CAB

KNOW IF IT WILL RAIN

THE EXPECTED OUTCOME

So I can

SATISFY MY HUNGER

FORGET ABOUT PARKING

TAKE AN UMBRELLA

USE "JOBS TO BE DONE" TO UNDERSTAND THE USER'S MOTIVATION

"Jobs to be done" is a very simple, yet very powerful template that reveals the user's motivation behind their actions. User motivation is a crucial information! Think about it, people don't want to buy features, but a solution to their problems. People don't want to buy four wheels and a shift gear, they want to easily get from point A to point B. People don't need the drill, they need the hole in the wall.

"Jobs to be done" is set to reveal the situation the user is in, let's say they are hungry. Then it analyzes the motivation and expected outcome to better understand the reason behind an action. This is how the template looks:
When I'm .... I want to .... So I can ....
I prepared a couple of examples on the left.

"Jobs to be done" is a natural way to reveal user motivation because of its sentence like format., so it can quickly easily reveal faulty logical threads.

User

ACTIONS

DETAILS

EMOTIONAL JOURNEY

DRAMATIC ARC

CHANNEL

THINKING

Download this free user journey map from uxbites.co

TOOLS FOR RESEARCH

THE USER JOURNEY MAP

User Journey maps are a highly valued tool in most design processes. They help to further understand the way users act, think and react to certain external factors. This gives a great insight on how to improve the customer experience, because it visually shows where the problem lies .

Each journey map is based around one persona and it's recommended to map all your personas separately.

Let's say you want to map how a user registers on your website. Write down all the steps they make to achieve that, under the "actions" section and give a note to each action under the "emotional journey" section. Connect the notes with a continuous line, which will reveal the emotional path of the user. It reveals when they are happy or when they are frustrated. When this is visualized, you will know exactly where you can still improve the process.

You can download this and other UX Research templates on uxbites.co for free!

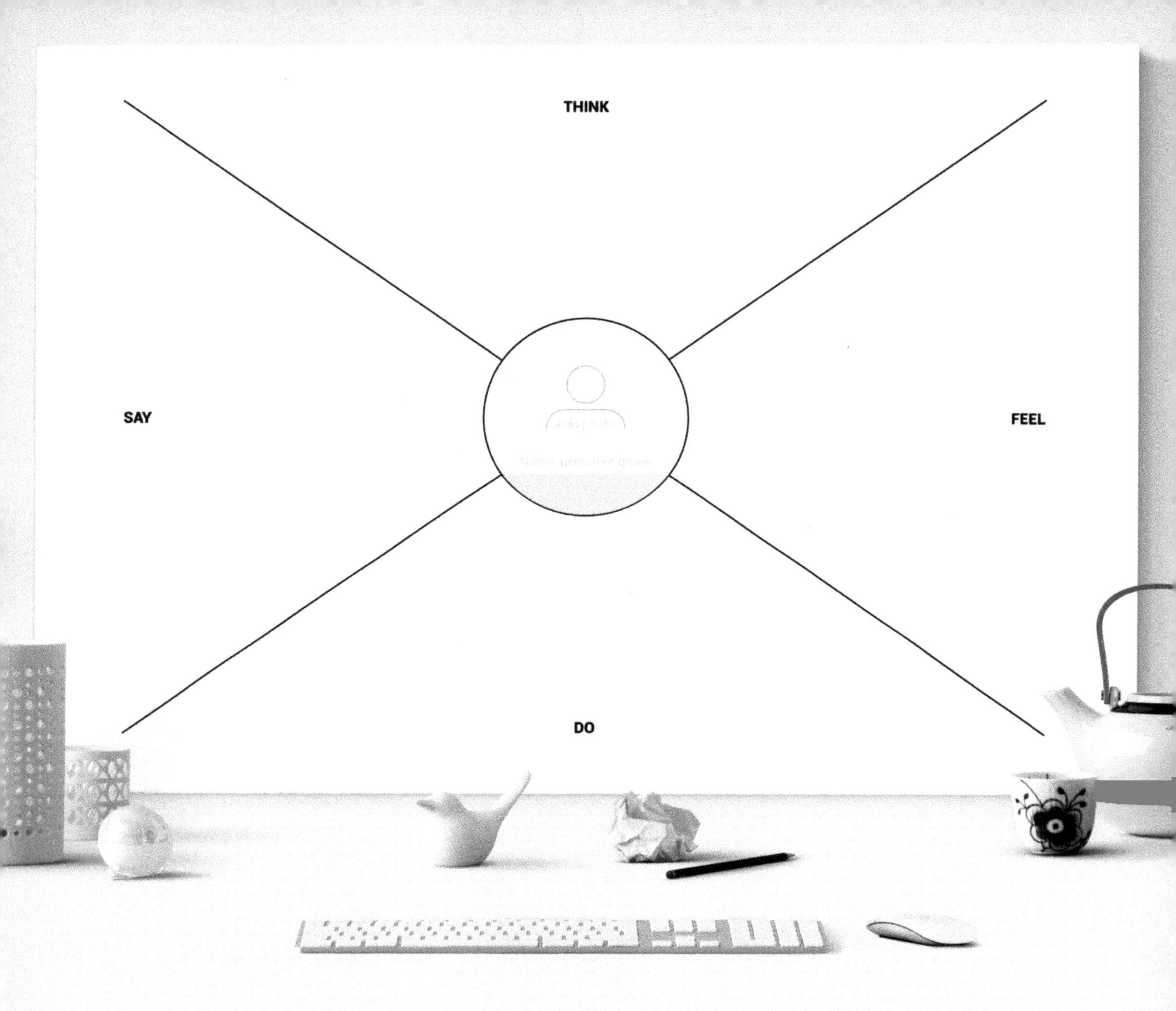

Download this free empathy map from uxbites.co

TOOLS FOR RESEARCH

EMPATHY MAP

Time to bring out all your sticky notes to play, you will need them for the empathy map!

Empathy maps are a great tool for visualizing user behavior and compare it with user attitude. Write on sticky notes what you know about the user, what they say, what they do, what they feel and what they think. When you're done, place each sticky note to the right section to clearly visualize where the user's frustration lies and how conscious they are of their pains. Each empathy map is based on a persona, because these factors differ depending on the target.

You should use the empathy map even if you don't have enough data on your users, map your speculations to organize your thoughts. Just don't forget that this is an ever changing map and you need to redo it when you have sufficient data at your hand.

You can download this and other UX Research templates on uxbites.co for free!

Where can I find User testers?

Already got a userbase? You're lucky!

A/B test multiple versions of you features or send out surveys, to get feedback from your people

Ask your client,

Who most probably know people from the target audience. Ask them to set up tests.

With Facebook ads!

You can look for testers via ads. A good targeted ad can bring you interested people, and you don't need many!

Usertesting.com

is the most well known platform. You can buy videos of a tester going through and commenting your platform and many other features but it's also the most expensive.

Buy user testers in your target

On platforms like Maze, Usabilityhub, Userlytics etc. you can buy any number of user testers from a well defined demographics, for relatively cheap.

The toughest part of user research must be finding the right user testers. And not just any kind of testers, but people from your niche, who are willing to test your ideas.
In fact, it doesn't need to be hard!

The easiest way to gather user testers is asking your client's help. They surely know people from the domain they are active, so ask them to find you a couple of willing testers. This will also make your client more involved in the process, which will make your direction much easier to sell!

On the left I gathered five main sources to find appropriate user testers. These days there are many platforms offering to find you testers in your niche, but the most obvious source is often forgotten. Your existing user base! If you already have that, you are lucky and you should definitely involve them! Asking your user's help will also mean a better acceptance for the upcoming change you are implementing.

PRACTICAL TIPS&TRICKS

FOR EVERY
UX DESIGNER

PRACTICE MAKES
PERFECT

LET'S GET PRACTICAL

We went through a couple of chapters talking about the nature of UX Design, which is best described as analytical. This means that context needs to be taken into consideration all the time, to make sure that you are designing for the right users and solving the right problems.

But there is a practical side to UX Design too! Best practices to follow, statistics to keep in mind, tips and tricks to apply in your process.
These general guidelines are shortcuts to satisfy your user's experience, so let's jump into them and savour each!

How we scan content

HOW USERS SCAN CONTENT

We should start this section by stating what we all know already, people don't spend much time reading on our platforms! They instead scan the content. They are looking for keywords about their interest.

Are you familiar with heatmaps? They're great tools out there that can follow your user's movement on pages and sum up the paths into a map that shows the hottest areas people focus on. First we realized how people scan content on the desktop, because smartphones weren't a thing in the time we were already using heatmaps. Research shows that people scan content on web pages in an F-shaped form, so the most important pieces of content should be placed in discoverable places.

But when smartphones appeared, we realized that F-shaped form were not lead by people's nature, but by the size of the screen. On smaller screens users focus at the center of the screen instead. That makes the two environments completely different, thus platforms shouldn't offer the same experience on both.

Most reachable areas

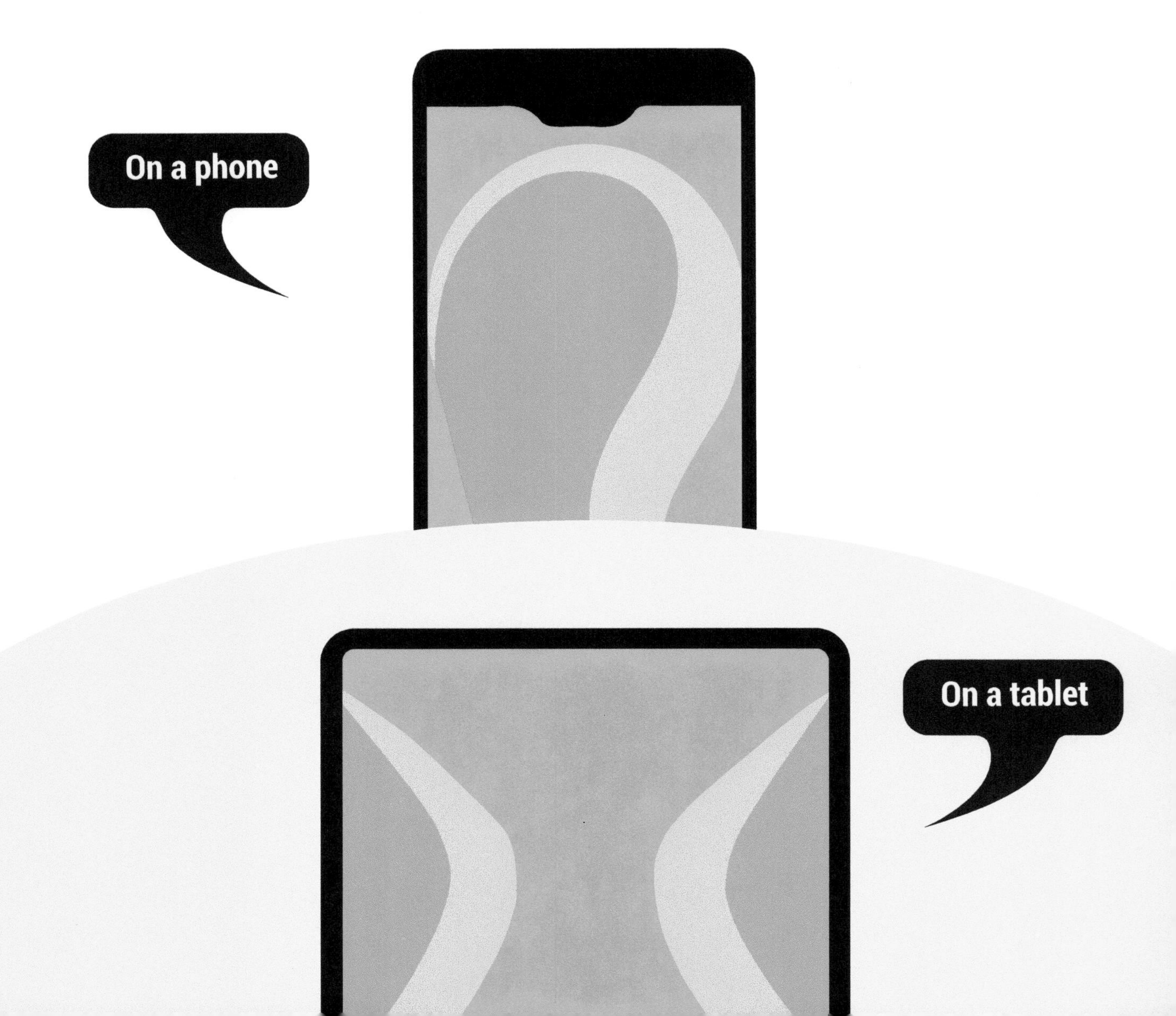

CONSIDER REACHABILITY

Reachability! Something we didn't have to consider until the appearance of smartphones, and later, tablets.

Research shows that 50% of the users hold their phones with one hand, which makes some areas harder to reach. This becomes more and more important as our screens grow in sizes. At the beginning, Android was placing their main navigation at the top, replicating the web experience, but as years went by, they moved the navigation at the bottom. Samsung's new UI guidelines also try to place everything that's important at the bottom of the screen, so it's easier to reach.

Of course, this is a totally different story on a tablet! People hold their tablets with two hands and that makes the center, which is the best place on phones, very hard to reach! That's why there are so many vertical navigation bars on tablet applications. This should also be a strong incentive to all designers to not just stretch out the phone app into a tablet version, because it's not going to be a great experience!

Meaning of the color red in different cultures

THINK ABOUT THE CULTURE YOU ARE DESIGNING FOR

Everybody knows Ebay, right? It's the biggest platform on the planet to sell second hand goods. It was a great success in the US and Europe and they decided to expand to China as well. They translated their website, but did nothing else to prepare the platform for a new culture. The project was a big failure and Ebay closed their Chinese division.

When was the last time you used QR codes? It never caught up in the US and Europe, but in China is the most frequently used payment method because it's cheaper than POS's.

Or look at how many connotations a color like red can have in different culture. All these examples should be a strong incentive to always respect the culture you are designing for!

Registration or checkout process?

Always ask sensitive information last!

PAY ATTENTION TO SENSITIVE INFORMATION

Your user doesn't have much time to waste and, while this makes grabbing their attention a challenge, it can also be used in your advantage!

The more time a user invests in your product, the smaller the chance that they will abandon it. This is something to keep in mind when designing longer processes like registration or checkout flows.

People think twice to give out their personal information and we will see later in the book that 34% of the users abandons checkout if they need to create an account. That's why it's recommended to always ask information that is potentially sensitive last!

Examples of scarcity in UX explained with your favorite sneakers

Just sold out!	VS	**Not available**
If you don't pick a product soon, you might loose all offers!		Since when? Don't show this if you can't explain why
Bought 10 times today	VS	**High demand today**
Meaning there'sa high demand for it		How high?
3 more left	VS	**Last pieces**
I should Hurry up!		Last 3? Last 100? It showed last pieces all day!
Offer Expires in 3 hours	VS	**Offer expires soon**
No time to waste!		I should buy this..soon

USE SCARCITY IN YOUR ADVANTAGE

This might not seem true, but the harder it is to get something, the more we want it!
People often link availability to quality and the fear of losing or missing out is a far bigger motivation than the wish of gaining. We call this scarcity!

The most obvious place to see scarcity tactics is in e-commerce and more specifically in travel and accommodation platforms. When we see that there are only three rooms left, our fingers are itching to not delay the booking. Or if we see that other people are watching a room too, we tend to action faster.

Having said that, note that scarcity techniques must always be based on true facts!
If you say that you have just three rooms left, it should be true, because scarcity is effective, but nothing is more important than the user's trust.

Also, don't say that the offer expires soon, because that can mean next week too! Use scarcity in your advantage but only if you can be specific!

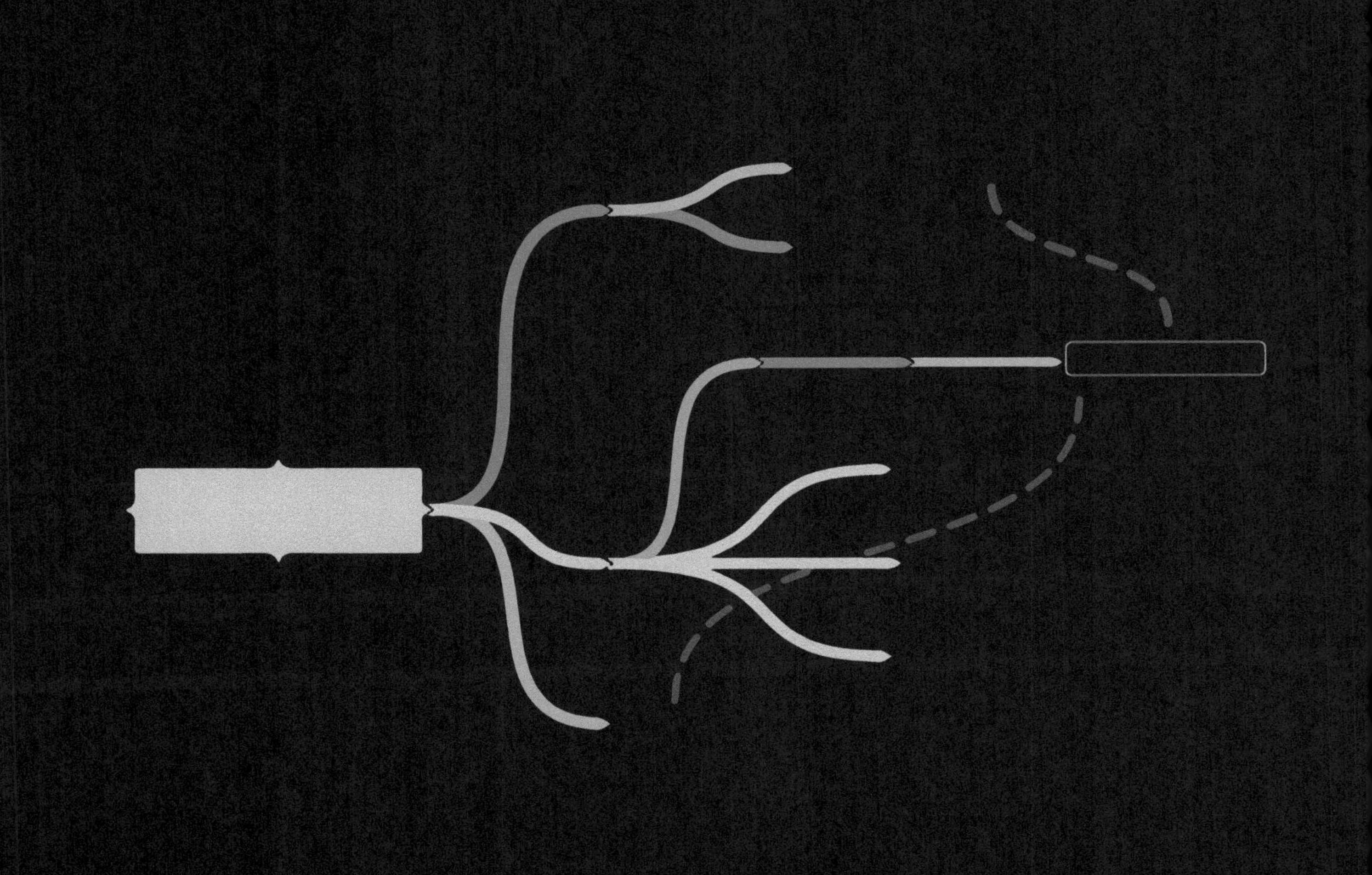

USING MIND MAPS FOR INFORMATION ARCHITECTURE

No, this is not the map of the New York Subway, but the map of a digital platform, often called the information architecture of a site or app.

Information architecture is very important because it helps to visualize all the pages of the platform, in connection with each other. This helps to reveal any redundancy you might have , but also missing screens.

UX Design is all about visualizing. Visualizing the user, their journey, their story, their pains, visualizing the architecture of the platform. You might think it's redundant and you have all the flow in your head, but most of the time drawing out the flow will reveal missing elements or logical flaws you should address before development.

It's also very easy to make! You can make it pretty, but it's not necessary, just sketch it on a paper or use platforms like Flowmapp, Wireflow, Coggle, Whimsical or Miro.

THE HOOK MODEL

TRIGGER
REWARD
ACTION
INVESTMENT

THE HOOK MODEL OR HOW TO FORM HABITS

Here's a bite on how habit forming products get you hooked and what makes us return to a platform over and over again.

The Hook Model is based on Nir Eyal's book called "Hooked, how to build habit-forming products" in which he explains in detail what are the four elements that can form habit. He defines Trigger, Action, Reward and Investment as the four factors to look for to form habits.

The model should be applied at the very beginning of each project, so it can help define the main reasons your product is potentially habit forming. It's also a great exercise to apply the model on well known platforms, to realize how they hook their users.

Let's look at the four habit-forming elements, in detail, on the next couple of pages!

Play video

Open e-mail

Ads

Download app

Notification

EXTERNAL

TRIGGER

INTERNAL

Memories

Routines

Friends

Situations

Places

Reacting to the the external or internal trigger,
the user takes action

Fullfills me

Makes me want more

Makes me come back

LONG TERM

User actions are valuable, but it doesn't guarantee that the user will be back to your platforms!

Offering instant or longterm rewards is a great way to keep the user coming back.

Sells something

Buys ticket

Pays bill

Finds answer

Makes me laugh

The final step into creating a habit-forming product is to make people invest time, energy and resources into your product.
The more a user invests into a platform, the most likely it is that they will return!

I invest in your platform and I will surely be back!

Contributing to platform

Share files

Create reputation

Connect with friends

PRACTICAL TIPS TO FOLLOW WHEN DESIGNING INTERFACES

The good thing about the analytical nature of UX Design is that platforms conduct numerous researches to realize what works and what doesn't. This approach to test and validate is certainly beneficial for each platform, but most of the research is also public! You can find countless valuable research made by the Nielsen Norman Group, so I suggest to check out their work.

In the next pages I gathered a couple of tips and tricks that are easy to understand and implement the next time you are working on related features and screens.

The general rule of UX Design is that you always need to design for the appropriate context, yet there are guidelines like these that you can safely follow, no matter the type or industry of the product. Let's dive in!

HIGHLIGHT IMPORTANT FEATURES BY PLACING THEM BETWEEN SIMILAR OR REPEATING ELEMENTS!

MORE CHOICES = LONGER TIME TO MAKE A DECISION!

CAN'T REDUCE CHOICES? BREAK THEM IN SMALLER STEPS!

USERS TEND TO REMEMBER THE FIRST AND LAST ITEMS FROM A LIST.

USE THIS FACT TO HIGHLIGHT WHAT'S MOST IMPORTANT!

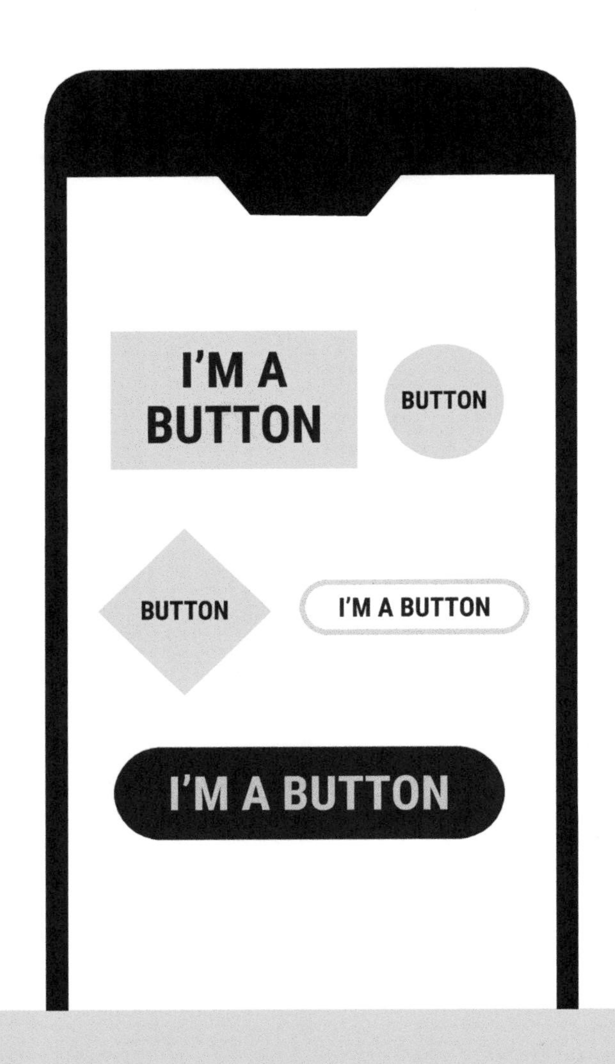

CONSISTENCY IS CRUCIAL! ALL BUTTONS SHOULD HAVE SIMILAR STYLE AND THEY SHOULD BE DIFFERENT FROM NON CLICKABLE TEXT.

THE MOST IMPORTANT ELEMENTS SHOULD BE AS LARGE AS POSSIBLE AND EASILY ACCESSIBLE WITH THE THUMB.

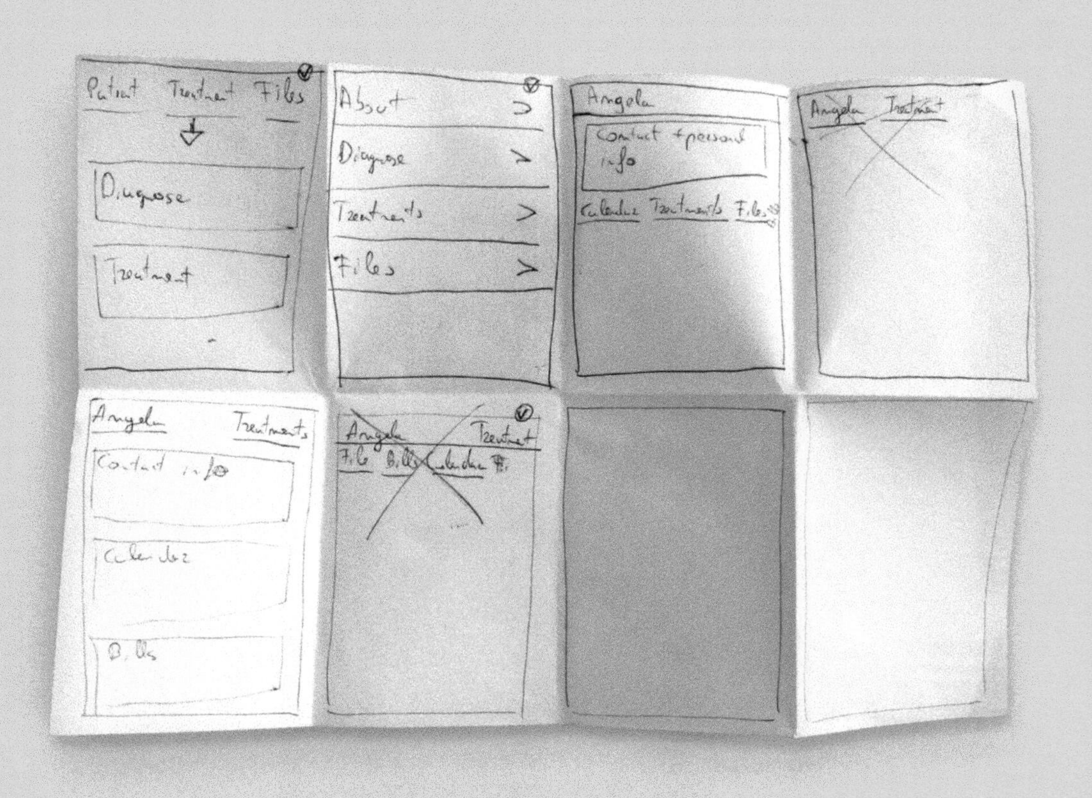
Patient Treatment Files
Diagnose
Treatment
About
Diagnose
Treatments
Files
Angela
Contact + personal info
Calendar Treatments Files
Angela Treatment
Angela Treatments
Contact info
Calendar
Bills
Angela Treatment

THE CRAZY 8 TECHNIQUE

The Crazy 8 technique is most commonly used in design sprints, but I think it's a great tool for individuals too. You can use it anytime you feel like you're out of ideas!

It's such an effective and fast paced way to come up with ideas. This technique will generate many directions and not all of them will work, but the ideas you've already sketched will inspire new ideas you haven't thought about before.

It's fun, it's fast, it's effective. Sounds perfect!

Here's how to do it: fold a paper in half, then in another half, then in half again, so you will get eight equal parts. Now set the timer for 8 minutes and start sketching!

Draw one idea per minute! There are no bad ideas, don't overthink it, just do it!

That's it. If you're doing this in a group, everybody will present their best ideas in the end and everybody will vote.

So you can see, the crazy 8 technique is a great way to generate new ideas, without overthinking them or being too judgemental with them.

Spotify, Netflix, Youtube

Great for consuming content

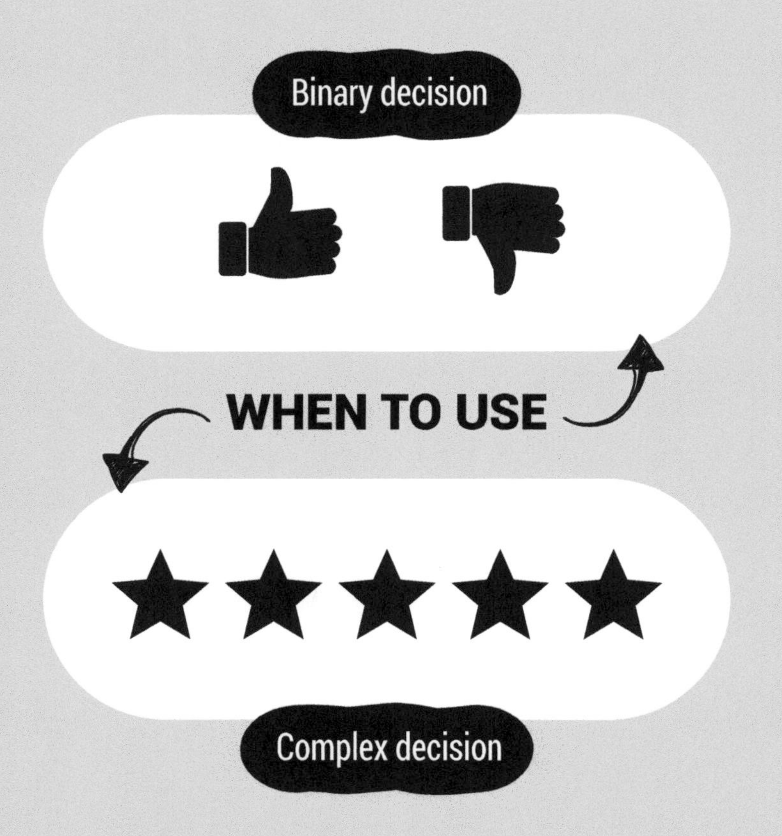

Great for helping buying decision

Online shops like Amazon or Service Rating like Uber

WHICH REVIEW SYSTEM TO USE

When we think about reviews, the first thing that comes in mind are five stars, but ratings with thumbs up or down is also a review system.

Now it's very natural that Youtube uses thumbs for reviews, but did you know that they too were using stars at the beginning? Netflix as well. Now both switched to thumbs up or down because it better suits their content! They realized that nobody was really giving 2,3 or 4 stars, only 1 or 5. People either loved or hated the content. So they turned to the thumbs system which resulted in a much higher engagement from the user and the reason is simple: it's a much faster process, therefore a smaller effort from the user's part.

This doesn't mean star ratings are out of date. They are still very powerful and beneficial in many platforms and there is still no better way to rate online shopping or services. Online shops use stars to help indecisive users, because star ratings also work as testimonials from real people, compared to marketing jargon.

LISTENING TO STATISTICS IN UX DESIGN

Understanding the value of User Experience Design and applying it accordingly can help prevent future issues, save time and money.

To demonstrate the value of this statement to anyone who might be skeptical, I prepared a couple of statistics to let the numbers speak for themselves.

This book can be summarized as a long advocacy for a research based design approach. And what does any research unravel if not data? Raw data won't convince anyone of the importance of UX Design but conclusions drawn from real data might!

Without further ado, did you know that ...

75%

of judgements on a site or app is based on aesthetics

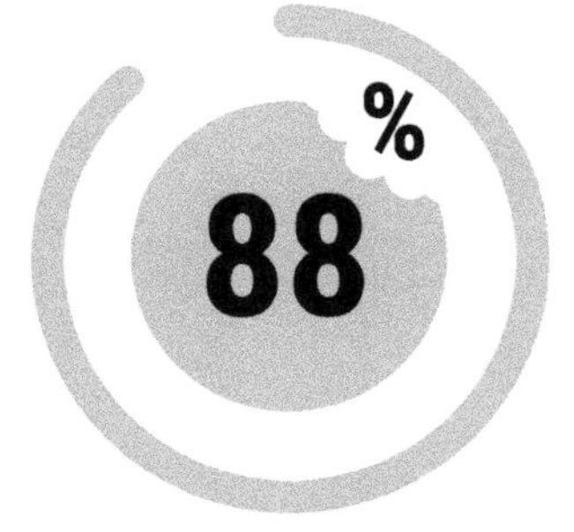

of users are less likely to return after a bad experience

of first impressions are design related

What's important for users

WHEN THEY USE A WEBSITE OR APP

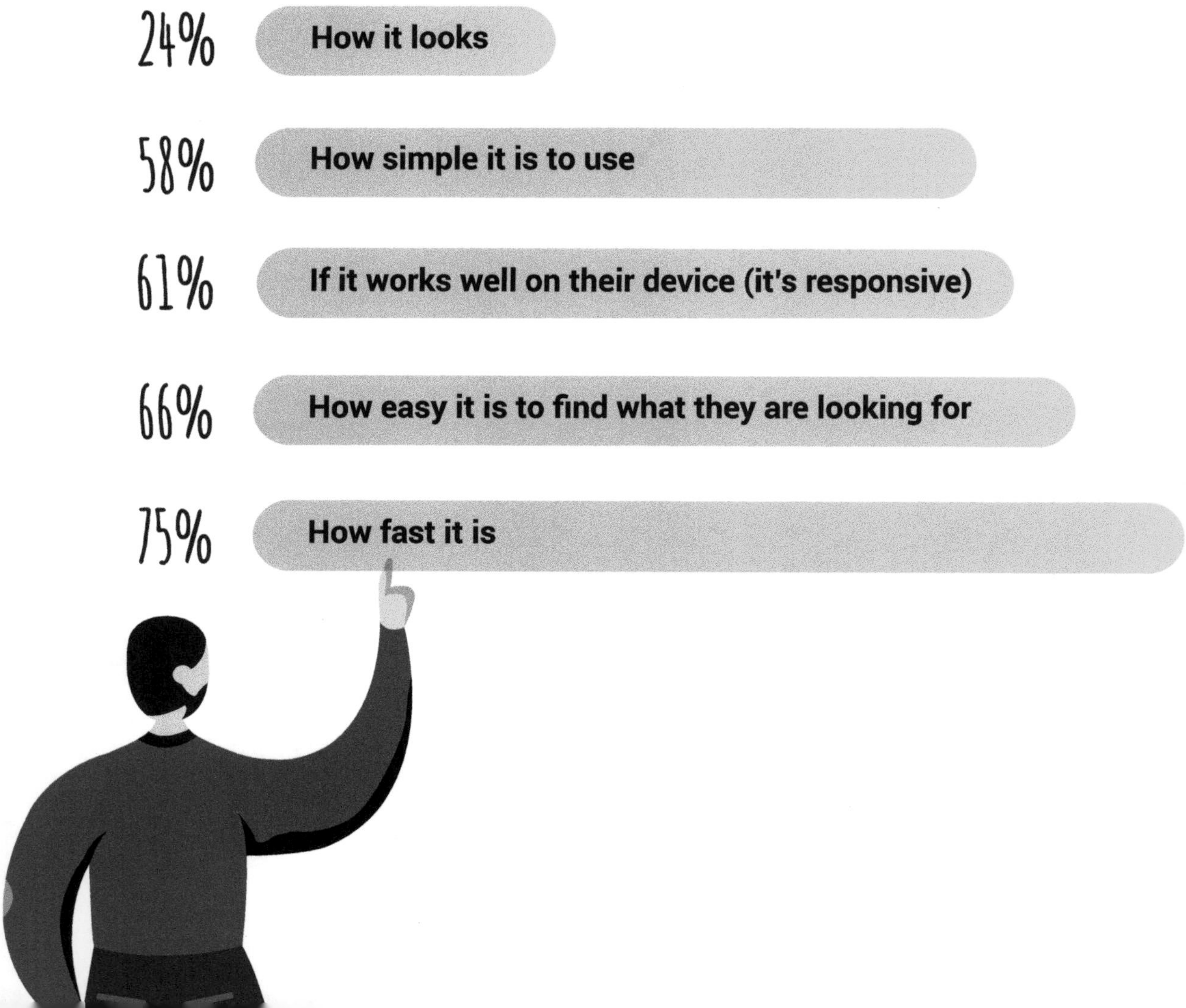

24% How it looks

58% How simple it is to use

61% If it works well on their device (it's responsive)

66% How easy it is to find what they are looking for

75% How fast it is

Reasons people ABANDON CHECKOUT

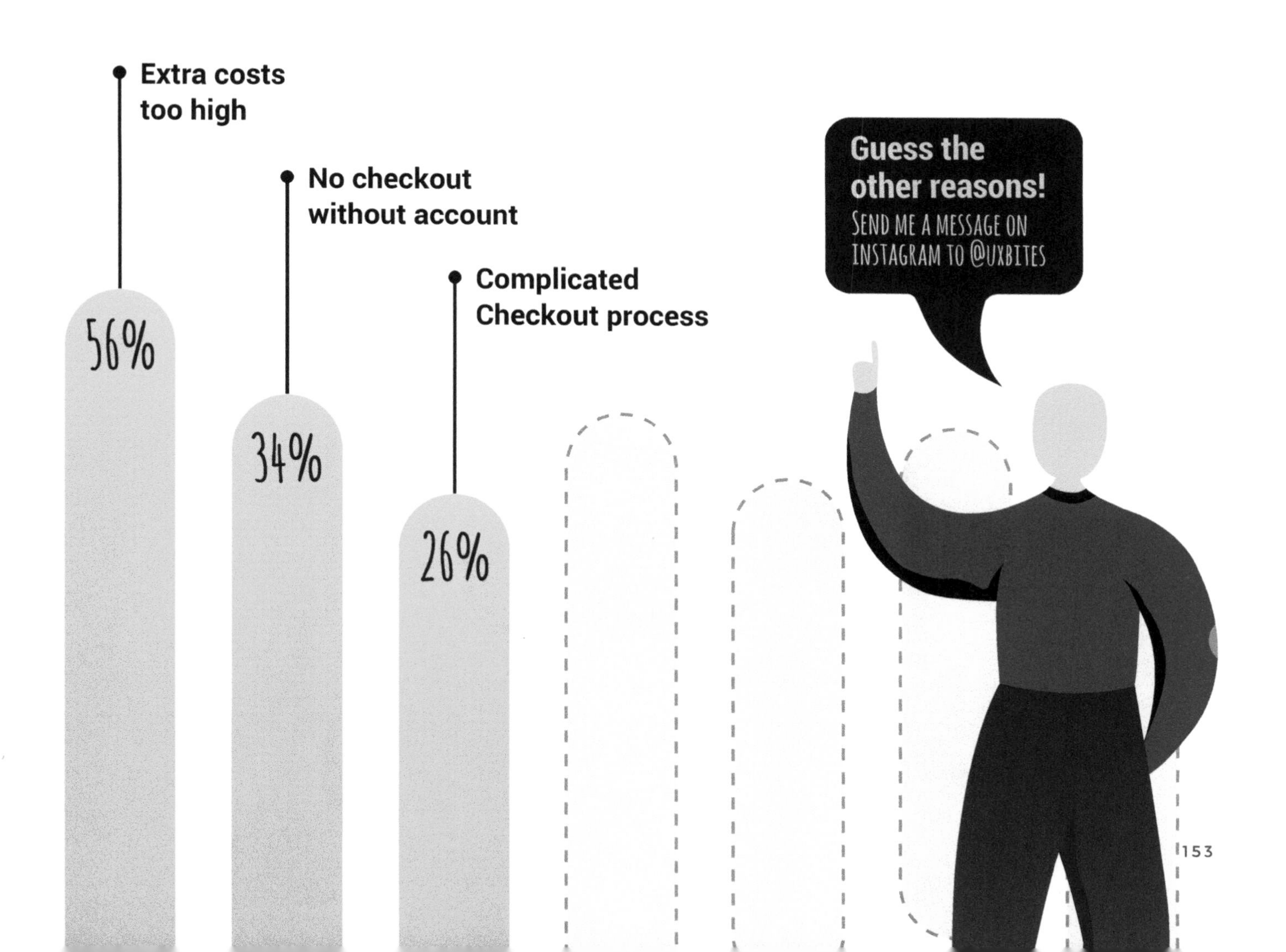

**BEAUTIFUL DESIGN
CAN MAKE USERS MORE TOLERANT
TO MINOR FUNCTIONALITY PROBLEMS**

5 Reasons to use Motion in UX

- Focus user attention the right place
- Creates context during page or object transitions
- Great way to show progress
- Makes navigation consistent
- A great incentive for interaction

MOTION IN UX DESIGN

Motion graphics brings to life static objects or characters to make us submerge in the dynamic world it creates. It's a powerful art form but in the context of UX Design, motion is something entirely different.

While it can be used to delight the user, motion in UX Design serves a functionality purpose. It can help to focus the user's attention to the right place, it shows progress, communicating that the system is working and it can offer incentive for interactions.

The main categories of motion in UX are micro interactions, page and object transitions and we will discuss each further on.

Using motion without a reason to helps usability can create an unnecessary distraction that might confuse users. That's why it's recommended to use motion only if it helps the user achieve their goal.

Being consistent with your motion approach is as vital as being consistent with your colors and typography. Similar elements should always animate the same way!

Loader types

INFINITE LOADER

For actions that take less than 10 seconds

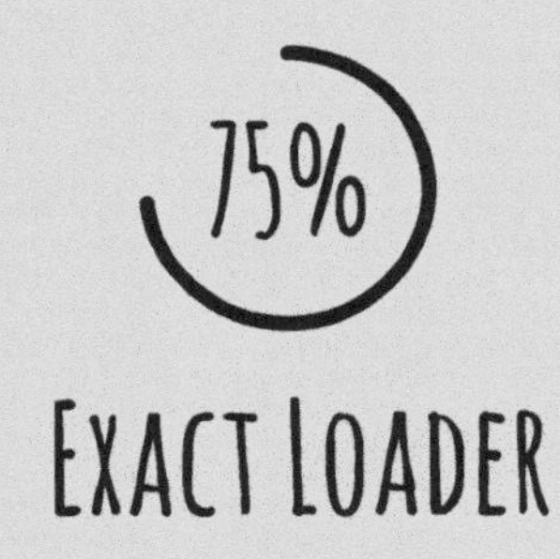

EXACT LOADER

For actions that take more than 10 seconds

- Don't use loaders for actions that take less than 1 second

- Explain why an operation can take longer

- For very long processes, offer a time estimate

MOTION IN UX: LOADERS

We might not be aware of the following statement, but loading animations couldn't be efficiently done without animation! There's just no way around this! Here's how to design the perfect loader for your project.

There are two main categories of loaders. Infinite loaders are usually an animation that doesn't show the exact progress, it just shows that the user's request is loading. This is ideal for loading times that are less than 10 seconds. Based on Jakob Nielsen's research, after 10 second, users will start to question if the request is working or not.

Precise loaders, on the other hand, show an exact or approximate progress. It shows the user that progress is happening so they trust that the system is working. This type of loading is ideal for processes that take more than 10 seconds. Additionally, if the process is very long, it's best to tell the users how much time it will take.

You don't have to use loaders for actions that are faster than a second. In these cases the loader just becomes a distraction.

Animation Speed Guide

Hover, fade and small objects

100MS

200MS

300MS

400MS

500MS

Large objects, page transitions

MOTION IN UX:
THE SPEED OF ANIMATION

We established why motion design is fundamental in UX Design. It's not something the user necessarily acknowledges and appreciate but they would feel frustrated from the lack of it.

The last vital factor to mention, when it comes to motion design, is the speed of the objects. Research shows that optimal animations should be between 200-500ms. Anything shorter than 100 ms can't be processed by our brain, we can't feel it, so it shouldn't be animated. On the other hand, anything longer than a second is interpreted as delay or latency.

The size of the elements are also an important variable. As in real life, bigger objects move smaller than smaller ones, and this principle should reflect the animation speeds in our interfaces. Smaller elements should move faster, large objects should move slower in order for them to feel natural.

Motion in UX Design is not about visual delight, but about guiding the user in their desired flow.

THE DARK SIDE

OF **UX**
DESIGN

DARK UX
Examples

GREAT POWER COMES WITH GREAT RESPONSIBILITY

The biggest part of the book focuses on the value and power of creating products with the user in mind. This is achieved with psychology, research and empathy. But psychology can also be used to manipulate people. When does hints and suggestions become tricks and mischiefs?

Dark Patterns in UX Design are unethical tricks used to nudge users into buying something they don't want making them sign up for something they didn't intended to.

Over the next couple of pages, let's look at a couple of examples of Dark Patterns in User Experience. These should help you understand what methods are generally considered frowned upon throughout the industry.

2567

NEW
APP

Sending way too much,
irrelevant notifications
(Notification Spam)

Plus pay weekly grooming for my dog

Dishonest or misleading
call to actions

"Confirmshaming"
or guilting the user into opting into
something

Psst, I'm actually an ad

Disguised ads trick user
into clicking them

I DON'T want to buy you a coffee every day
Unexpected behaviour:
opts-out users only if they check the box

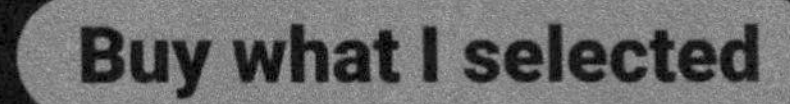

Buy with extra upgrade

Nudging users to buy something
they did not express to buy

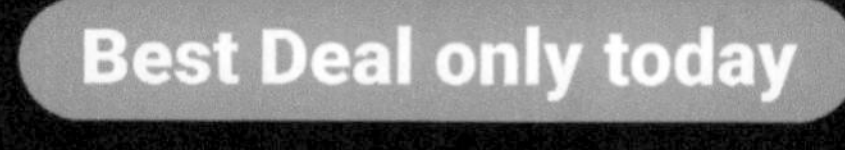

And the rest of the year

Creating urgency with
dishonesty, like limited offer or last item in stock.
(use it only if it's true)

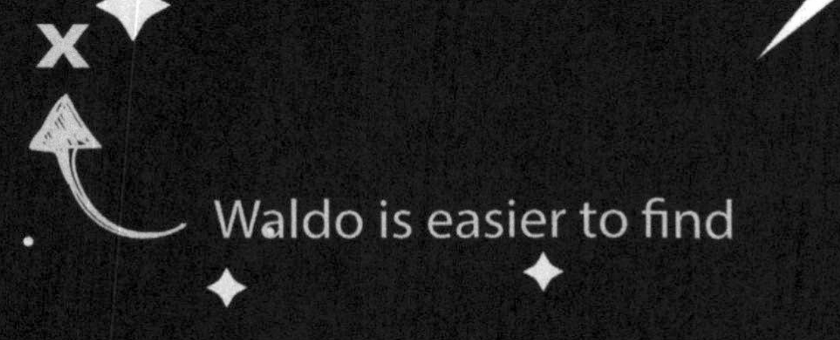

See our offer

Barely noticable opt-out option

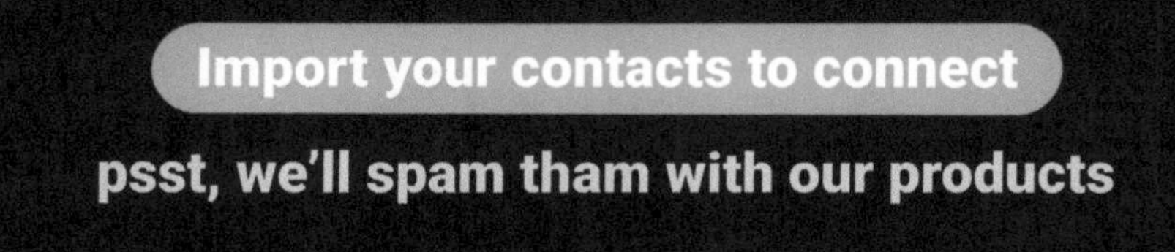

Being dishonest about
the consequences of an action

Guiding the user's attention is the main goal of User Experience Design, but guidance is just one step away from misleading and deceptive behavior. The difference between the two example is the purpose of the project. One tries to serve the user's needs, which will lead to an organic desire for the product, while the other tries to trick users which might lead to short term gain but also to a stained brand.

Dark patterns exploit psychology to get users to do things they never wanted to do.

Be aware that as the web becomes more and more regulated, dark patterns won't be only unethical but against the law too. A successful platform these days can be built and maintained only with honesty.

THANK YOU!

You made it to the end of the book! Or maybe just opened it here. Either way, this is the last page that I write so it really feels like the end of it for me.

This book was corrected by my girlfriend who was patient enough to go through all the industry jargon, so I want to thank her in the first place. I also want to thank to all the beautiful people from the @uxbites instagram page, who showed their interest for this book. Their support pushed to move forward and release it.

I hope you find this book useful enough to recommend it to your fellow designer friends, and if not, drop by at @uxbites on instagram and tell me all about it!

Don't forget to take a photo in your feed or story and tag @uxbites so I can share your experience with the community! See you there!